JOURNAL OF A NORTH DEVON NATURE LOVER

Observations and Reflections on Flora and Fauna

Stewart Beer

Edward Gaskell *publishers*
DEVON

First published in 2000 by
Edward Gaskell *publishers*
Unit 7 Caddsdown Business Park
Bideford
Devon EX39 3DX

ISBN: 1 - 898546 -37 -1

JOURNAL OF A NORTH DEVON
NATURE LOVER

Observations and Reflections
on Flora and Fauna

Printed & Bound by
Lazarus Press
Unit 7 Caddsdown Business Park
Bideford
Devon EX39 3DX

To that *solacing thought* :
The Council for the Protection of Rural England
CPRE
expounding the villainies of blotting and smothering
our open countryside

He stops, as one unwilling to advance,
without another, and another glance. . .
With what a pure and simple joy he sees
those sheep and cattle browsing at their ease!
Easy himself, there's nothing breathes or moves
but he would cherish; —all that lives he loves.

from 'The Borough'

George Crabbe

By the same author

An Exaltation of Skylarks
(published SMH Books, Pulborough West Sussex)

An Earthlife Anthology
(Volturna Press, Hythe Kent)

Nature alone is antique, and the oldest art a mushroom
Carlyle

CONTENTS

INTRODUCTION

Myopic planners and developers are requisitioning our pastoral Eden at an alarming rate; just at the time when we need an escape from the pressures and tensions of the modern age.

It seems the poets of old had a vision of the kaleidoscopic edifices which twentieth and twenty first century man would dump on his environment. And ever more road building schemes—those open wounds on the face of our countryside.

> Is then no nook of England
> secure from rash assault ?
>
> *William Wordsworth*

We must wrest these piratical hands from the landscape. The watchword in determining our way forward should be 'we are the children of nature, not its master.' Let us be vigilant, and hence worthy benefactors, and preserve a vital legacy for generations to come.

> God has lent us the earth for our life. It is a great entail. It belongs as much to those who come after, as to us, and we have no right, by anything we do or neglect, to involve them in any unnecessary penalties, or deprive them of the benefit which is in our power to bequeath.
>
> *John Ruskin* (1819–1900)

It is the simple pleasures which prove the most rewarding: to be in tune with nature conveys a lasting harmony with the inner self.

> A man is rich in proportion
> to the number of things
> he can let alone
>
> *Henry Thoreau*

This diary does not purport to be anything other than its title implies: brief notes on some of the natural history to be seen in the seasons of the year, made in the North Devon area where I have lived since birth; an area I shall never seek to trade. And, although I am hardly likely to lay a formal treatise at the door of science, being an ardent observer of the local scene has developed in me an insight that is warming in its rewards.

> A rich domain,
> presenting a lifetime's absorption!

During my youth Lord Grey of Fallodon (see *The Charm of Birds*) and Henri Fabre (*Souvenirs Entomologiques*) in pursuit of their studies in a corner of their respective homeland, made a lasting impression.

> Men that undertake only one district
> are more likely to advance natural knowledge
> than those that grasp at more than
> they can possibly be acquainted with:
> every kingdom, every province,
> should have its own monographer.
>
> *Gilbert White*

When I was six years of age my parents bought me the illuminating ten-volume *Pictorial Knowledge*. These books were to inspire me to a lifetime's interest in nature. Volume 2 set the stage with enthralling accounts on Darwin's voyage in the *Beagle* and Walter Henry Bates's Amazonian escapades. Luminaries elsewhere too of naturalists and poets. In Volume Seven I came across a brief biography of the eminent naturalist-poet Richard Jefferies. However, many years were to elapse before I could lay my hands on copies of his works.

And what a revelation they turned out to be: Jefferies surely is the bright star in the firmament of nature writers. He was born at Coate Farm in the hamlet of that name in North Wiltshire and, although in his thirties he left to live near London, his spirit always remained here. I have quoted from him freely throughout this book.

It is many times more important to feel as to know.

The discovery of nature's treasure banishes insipidity and tedium and an impregnable level of contentment is attained through eyes that have learnt to see. This new elevation of the spirit prevails over every mundane matter. Each subsequent day is endorsed by new experiences in the ever-changing living tapestry that is our countryside.

> I am monarch of all I survey,
> my right there is none to dispute.

William Cowper

. . . yet our unsullied landscape is increasingly threatened by bricks and mortar.

If we could only grasp that we are a part of—and not apart from—the natural world, then maybe we could meet the vaunted Shangri-la.

> What is this life if, full of care,
> we have no time to stand and stare?

To ward off the canker of insensitivity those words, from the poem 'Leisure' by the Super-Tramp poet W. H. Davies, should be engraved on our minds. And in this machine-embroiled age the lines have the resonance of ocean rollers or the crystal fluting of the song thrush on our jaded ears.

> Accuse not nature, she hath played her part;
> Do thou but thine, and be not diffident of
> Wisdom, she deserts thee not, if thou
> Dismiss not her.

John Milton

The essential character of the naturalist is unsuppressible love, burnished by an enduring patience. Patience to remain motionless, merging into the pastoral scene, whereupon nature, so deceived, lets slip her veil. Then, with the observer's senses honed raptor keen, her exquisite features are gradually revealed.

Countless are the hours I have thus spent, where for that time the society of man is subsumed by nature (though thoughts of his compulsion to desecrate the countryside abide to score across the mind).

> The fields his study; nature was his book.
>
> *William Hazlitt*

From an early age I have been imbued with the harmony and bliss drawn from nature's shrine. I remember well, when I was four, my father holding me up to peer into the hawthorn hedge. The first sight of the New World could not have moved Columbus more than my discovery of the turquoise-blue eggs in the dunnock's nest. That revelation was to give me a lasting deep delight in nature.

> To her fair world did nature link
> The human soul that through me ran;
>
> from 'In Early Spring'   *William Wordsworth*

A gyrating diversity under cyclic control.

By the dictates of the universal laws our planet both revolves upon its axis and orbits the sun. And from interstellar collisions were the building blocks of life ignited.

A vast chain of being!

A synchrony of movement. Darkness and light. The moth and the butterfly. Warming and cooling. Seasonal migration. The emergence of a mayfly. And worlds within worlds: a droplet of water is a teeming (microscopic) metropolis of life . . .

> Everything in nature acts in
> conformity with law.
>
> *Immanuel Kant*

The flowing transition of the seasons could not be better ascribed than to these verdant isles of ours.

Nature abhors a vacuum.

Françoise Rabelais

A diary record of natural history encounters invites an absorbing reflection in the years ahead. From each entry memories will gather, bringing back to life those unique moments of their inception. Who knows what potent event may disclose itself to the quiet watcher and, lucidly written, become preserved in detail for future delectation?

Beatae memoriae

The secret of all living creatures is . . . quiet.

Richard Jefferies

JANUARY

ustere winter opens the calendar year. Those enjoying invigorating expeditions into the countryside are sometimes waylaid by the mordant potency of the elements. Winging down from the chill penury of northerly latitudes to a roost on the edge of our market town are five long-eared owls. Coincidentally, a short-eared owl has taken up residence nearby—on expansive wings a day-time foray across the splash-meadow leaves the watcher in awe. In the estuary a great northern diver, and on the pocket of moorland, hen harriers . . .

Conditions can influence fortunes by the hour. On a rare day comes the unexpected luscious sweet scent of the winter heliotrope, conjuring up a vision of summertime hedgerows frothy with meadowsweet. However, the very next day every trace is lost to the winds that now agitate the most stalwart of trees.

Over the years, frost and ice, often the most effective agents of erosion, find a course into first the branch and later the bole of a diseased or storm-rent tree, and, with the added attention of summertime heat and the activities of wood-boring insect larvae, its days are numbered. High winds, perhaps close-heeled to heavy rainfall, then stage the final act, toppling the condemned to the now unshaded earth. And oh, how the elms are missed.

A blanket of snow impedes the feeding rooks and wood pigeons. Hitherto, barley corn-shoots were taken but now horticulturists had better beware: early sown broad beans and, best of all, *Brassicae* are apt to be taken à la carte. In the extreme conditions occurring in the winter of 1962/63—the worst for 200 years—I witnessed a gang of piratical rooks, with carrion crows in close support, bring down and rip apart an injured—or starving—herring gull.

Stationed on its customary gorse sprig the pert cock stonechat provides a welcome contrast to the drab backcloth. A black head and white collar swiftly identifies *Saxicola*, a quite common bird wherever there is scrubland.

On a particular occasion I was trudging my way through snow alongside a gorse-clad bank bordering a conifer plantation when suddenly I caught a glimpse of a tiny, wren-like bird, darting in and out of the undergrowth and hence eluding identification. Running forward to where it had last dipped into the bushes I peered eagerly, but saw no trace of it.

Somewhat deflated I turned away, thinking I would not see the mysterious bird again—but there it was, a moment later, continuing its tantalising flight. After a few moments with me in dogged pursuit, the little fellow decided to stand to be recognized. For my benefit and delight it perched on a protruding twig and I saw that it was in fact a goldcrest.

I have seen many of these exquisite birds since those far off days of my youth but, I wonder, shall I have to indulge in the same game if (or when) I register my first firecrest?

During the summer months, when the birdwatcher's statue-still form is obscured by surrounding foliage the smaller birds pay little heed to his presence. On one occasion, when standing next to a drooping oak branch I was so close to a goldcrest it could have seen its reflection in my eyes. Titmice, warblers and the wren are a good example of this but, during wintertime, when the landscape is divested of its leafy robes, most, with the possible exception of nuthatch and tree creeper, are far more difficult to stalk—unless, that is, very cold weather prevails to make times even leaner than usual.

On another cold January morning, whilst traipsing across the countryside with the aim of sighting the locally attached flock of lapwings, I suddenly heard a 'tap-tapping' emanating from a stack of ash poles recently cut from the hedge on which they were leaning. I quickened my pace in lively expectation, and nearing the stack, I saw that the sound was being made by a workman-like great spotted woodpecker. Beautiful. Hoping for a more detailed inspection I stealthily approached until I could have stretched out my hand to it. For what seemed like minutes, though it was almost certainly no more than a few seconds, I stood transfixed.

The woodpecker, a female, chipped methodically at the bark of one of the poles, then, still unaware of my presence, flew off across the field in typical swooping style. My pleasure at this close encounter was tinged with regret that I had not had a camera at hand for what could have been an impressive shot, and visual proof of my stalking proficiency. Great spotted woodpeckers have shown a distinct liking for the beech trees in the area and many, including saplings, are riddled with their trademark holes to bear this out. Of course sap itself is a predilection of theirs.

The bird order *Corvidae* (crows), incorporating rook, magpie, jackdaw, jay and carrion crow, strut or hop along the frost-hardened arable land and search with piercing eye for worms, grubs and the occasional insect and ear of corn. The rook is notably beneficial to farmland, accounting for innumerable 'leather-jackets', the larvae of the crane fly or daddy-long-legs, which would otherwise inflict serious damage.

It can be noted at this time of year that these usually wary birds become comparatively bold, the appeasement of hunger taking precedence over the fear of man. Thus observation is made all the easier. However, when approaching a flock of rooks that holds a pair of magpies or even a solitary jay, the latter are the first to take flight. "Chack chack" is the departing cry of the colourful jay and, with equal alacrity, the magpies dip arrow-like over the tree-lined hedge, there to continue a rude "chivvying", obscured from the interloper.

In common with other corvids the rook is sharp and opportunistic, as the following account testifies:

In my home village our garden backed on to open countryside, thus attracting to the lawn great numbers of birds and varieties of species. The rook, however, although gregarious among its own, is usually far too wary to venture so close to the abode of man. But one, I noticed, came regularly to perch in the apple tree at the far end of the garden, to remain motionless until some hapless bird, usually a starling or house sparrow, flew in that direction with a beakful of food.

Then, as the unsuspecting carrier rounded the apple tree, the rook would launch into a surprise mid-air confrontation, causing the startled bird to cry out in panic and drop the prize. The assailant swiftly retrieved and ate the surrendered titbit, returning to the same position in readiness for the next course. A country version of skua versus gull if ever there was.

The carrion crow has adapted to methods and haunts which also illustrate the crow family's intelligence. *Corvus corone* has learnt to eke out a living in and around towns. I know of one particular pair that year after year have raised their offspring in a nest on a small industrial estate. How quickly they learnt to scavenge for scraps of bread around the factories. And how loyal they were to their progeny, supporting them throughout the bleak winter months.

On the shingle beach, who knows which bird was it, herring gull or carrion crow, that first took a mussel in its bill, to fly to a height of twenty metres to release the potential meal over the rocks below in order to crack open the shell . . . ..

"Ho-hoo-hoo-ooooo!" The tawny owl's hoots are an integral part of the starry pastoral night: "Hu . . . witt!" replies its mate. Old country folk used to remark on the 'night hawk's' presence—pervasive sounds to the ear of the country-lover. But the spectral form, stealing down the lane, has become a rare feature for the late-night excursionist—the barn owl population has dipped precipitously.

Let us hope the European Union's latest dictates will return farming in general to being sympathetic and in harmony with nature, and that this will restore to the barn owl the habitat which has been so wantonly ploughed under or levelled.

Sometimes it seems that every other field harbours flocks, in varying size, of fieldfares and redwings. For me, these attractive Scandinavian thrushes are to winter what the swallow is to summertime—intrinsic and precious.

Cones of Scot's pine, collected by children after the previous day of high winds have wrenched them free from inaccessible branches, quickly open out in response to indoor temperatures. Here is a splendid opportunity to muse on the ingenuity of certain birds to extract the seeds from this coniferous fruit.

The second day of the new year 1996 brought a light south to sou'westerly breeze, teasing warm air on to the peninsula. On the saltmarsh groups of linnets and skylarks feed on the seeds of sea purslane which line the channels lying parallel or conversely at ninety degrees to where the river and estuary converge where, during the run, salmon are sometimes found stranded. A linnet is observed skilfully snipping a postage-stamp-size portion of shiny leaf off a sea beet plant. Water droplets from the previous evening's shower cling to the foliage and the feeding birds quickly become sodden.

The twittering groups of linnets fly to the hawthorns and poplars growing beyond the highest reaches of the tide and here they preen and dry their plumage before returning to another session of feeding. How important the plantlife of the estuary is . . .

Concentrated here are many wildfowl, waders in particular: the area fairly pulses with avian sights and sounds. The abrupt trills and calls of curlew pervade the atmosphere and an individual is seen wading belly-deep in the receding tidal water. A scaup surfaces close to the mudbank and is given a cursory eye from the redshank thereon. Further down the estuary dunlin and ring plover dash along the shingled beach, probing hither and thither, and an accompanying turnstone walks methodically from pebble to pebble.

Nearby, a little egret—there are at present over twenty-five hereabouts—rises from the water's edge and wafts away upstream, then veers inland to settle in the field ditch. Childlike pleadings are the cries of 'peewit'. Large numbers of lapwing and golden plover consort along the waterline.

Overhead arrive yet more lapwings and from the main body two or three birds shoot out and tumble, giving an unexpected preview of the wildly exuberant spring display flight.

In a pine forest in search of crossbills (and possibly hawfinches and bramblings) during another unseasonably warm day I took an old footpath through a mature light-screening section of plantation. The thinly scattered bramble and heather plants incarcerated here were seen to be woefully checked in growth. 'Outside' a strong breeze whipped the tops of the pines, releasing into the stillness below a steady stream of needles and particles of bark to a yielding ground.

Jarred from hibernation a small tortoiseshell butterfly weaved an aerial course through the maze of trunks and was quickly lost to sight. In the marshy forest clearing a brief hour of sunlight drew a cloud of midges. A goldcrest that had been feeding in the upper branches of the larch suddenly realised the bounty before it and made repeated sallies into their midst. Suddenly it was confronted by another of its kind and a skirmish ensued, whereon both birds disappeared, to leave the midges to the joys of warmth and light. A natural Christmas tree display: tassels of cones festoon the upper branches of the Norway spruce and beckon crossbills (alas, there are none abroad . . .)

SEVERE WEATHER

1776, January—exceptionally mild
1814, 1881—great snowstorms
1825, 19th July—thermometer at 99° F—grampuses at Penhill
    (from *Memorials of Barnstaple*, Joseph Besley Gribble 1830
                 reprinted by Edward Gaskell *publishers* 1994)
1879/1882—appalling weather throughout: endless rain
    (from *The Diary of S.G. Kendall*, Westcountry yeoman farmer
     British farming brought to the edge of collapse)
1881—48hr blizzard
1893—very little rain between February and July
1910, 16th December—North Devon storm
1952, 15th August—Lynmouth disaster
1962/63—snowbound winter
1976, July/August—drought
1978, February—blizzard

The drought of '95 was followed by an autumnal bounty of mushrooms, fruit and seeds—as was the case after the preceding drought of '76. Sloes hung like grapes and there was a glut of acorns and beechmast. Wood pigeon flocks were noticeably absent in many parts in early winter as the birds kept to the woodlands to feast. Garden birds were also low in attendance through the second half of that year; until mid-January, when the countryside fare was exhausted.

Even having taken into account the dearth of a wide range of plant and insect life there is still a great deal to observe and to enjoy. Much of the birdlife concentrates in certain areas and this presents the sedentary watcher many weeks of rewarding observation.

The amplified trills of a curlew under a defunct concrete jetty focuses the eyes to the long legged, long billed wader, posturing aggression at another of its kind, which responds by stepping backwards at a tangent. A turnstone flies out and away from the altercation. (Was it its mate that was taken close by a week ago by a peregrine?) The feathers plucked off a wood-pigeon strewn on and under the stump of an ash in the woodland clearing evidence the kill of a sparrow hawk or, just maybe, a goshawk!

Winter and the dark embrace of death . . .

From the middle of the month there is a gradual lengthening of daylight: the spell of spring will soon be cast. Silvery tufts start to show on the developing anthers of the sallows. Some of the resident birds begin to pair up. Almost a blur the frenzied chirping mass of house sparrows spin along the ground—the skittish fleeing from the enamoured. Darting past with excited chatter the blackbird sees off a prospecting suitor of its mate. And on the rooftop a pair of starlings are engrossed in ritual courtship. The nesting season draws ever nearer . . .

Heraldic snowdrops form botanic drifts in the winter wilderness. Like the snowdrop, some of the earliest plants to show are also the most fragile in structure, the primrose and celandine to name but two, a fact that never fails to elicit wonder.

Dynamic Earth and atmosphere:
now global warming seems a reality
when next another Ice Age to impinge our shores?

THE SNOWDROP

From hidden bulb the flower reared up
Its angled, slender, cold dark stem,
Whence dangled an inverted cup
From tri-leaved diadem.

Walter de la Mare

FEBRUARY

If February give much snow
A fine Summer it doth foreshow.

English rhyme

ebruary advances with the first tangible signs of coming spring following in its wake. In open spaces the beloved skylarks, ever jubilant, rise heavenwards—to the 'welkin's crest'—singing their paeans of praise. Soon rich melody issues from the bare-limbed trees: blackbird, song and mistle thrush, wren and dunnock in full voice—for our utmost enjoyment. The robin's sweet clear whistle is heard in garden, hedgerow and woodland. And I shall always remember the first audience with a wren's 'song-burst'. I was indeed taken aback by the power of the little bird's delivery.

JENNY WREN

'Twas then she burst, to prove me wrong,
Into a sudden storm of song;
So very loud and earnest, I
Feared she would break her heart and die.

W. H. Davies

Rooks voice a clamorous, tuneless welcome, yet blithely at one with the symphonies of dawn and dusk.

Sooth'd by the genial warmth, the cawing rook
Anticipates the spring.

Gilbert White

In the garden, the leaves of crocus and daffodil extend upwards apace: yet these are grossly uncertain days, with the weather lurching from sunny mildness to ferocious storm, with bitter northern winds . . .

> If Candlemas Day be fair and bright,
> Winter will have another flight;
> But if Candlemas Day be clouds and rain,
> Winter is gone, and will not come again.

Because of the scarcity of small mammals in the throes of winter, the nocturnal barn owl has had to extend its hunting activities into the daylight hours in order to gain its fill. Before dusk and late into the morning it may be seen quartering, or fanning, kestrel-like, over a stretch of field, hoping to snatch an unwary prey.

An interesting feature at this time is the local rook populace, congregating in an appointed field to begin their courtship routine which, for the unattached, culminates in a choice of partner. There is a rubbing together of bills, seabird style, interspersed with unison springs off the ground. After this ritual, when pairing has taken place, the flock heads back to inspect the rookery, to be greeted noisily, as ever, by those already in occupancy.

Old nests are used time and time again but, having been exposed to the brunt of winter, repair work is often required before the re-lining of the interior and the laying of eggs. It is not unusual to espy newly paired rooks nest-building over a vacated site, with, in time, a further five or six nests constructed over the original—the bird world's version of the tenement block. Purloining of sticks from adjacent nests seems fair play to the homemakers and initiates many a cacophonous skirmish.

Exquisite clumps of primroses clad the mossy bank. Day on day, millimetre by millimetre the soft, yellow catkins lengthen to eventually fill in the hazel bough spaces. In a sheltered aspect the red campion has survived the rigours of winter and is visited by the first eager scouts of the dormant— or yet to be born—insect hordes. On a south-facing bank the rich sheen on the lesser celandine is a glinting proclamation of the miracle of growth and beauty—just a few weeks ago this plant was no more than a tuberous root. Here also the wild strawberry plants hug the drying ground.

Nearby, a lizard blinks as it relishes the fleeting radiance. Above the bank, beech trees rustle as their few remaining crisp, russet leaves catch each fitful breeze. Now, dried leaves and grasses are at a premium, to be sought as ideal material for nest building bird and mammal and utilised with amazing skill.

In the unhoed vegetable garden a few groundsel, germander speedwell, ground ivy and red deadnettle linger. In ditch and stream the black-dotted, glutinous masses of frog-spawn lie in peril from sharp-eyed birds. On the high moor, the buffeting wind has lifted, then rolled, the spawn from the shallow, water-filled ruts and depressions on to the heather clumps.

When hatched, the tadpoles first exist on a diet of aquatic vegetation. However, with advancing growth, and seeking the safety of deeper water, they begin to prey on invertebrate denizens. Great losses are sustained throughout their development—and not solely from jar-toting youngsters (and their parents). I have watched carrion crows feeding on tadpoles from a roadside ditch; ducks and herons too, are eager to partake. After some twelve weeks the tadpoles have formed into froglets and, leaving the water, the thumb-nail sized creatures seek shelter in the grass tussocks and herbage of the water meadow or pond fringe. Skin shedding accommodates the creatures further stages of growth—another illustration of nature's remarkable innovative life-cycles.

During this month the milder, sunshine-blessed days can be graced with the first appearance of the small tortoiseshell and peacock butterflies, both having survived hibernation and all its attendant dangers. The former has ventured out from the comparative safety of garden shed or outbuilding. One may come across many of its kind which didn't make it into the new year, lying dead on floor or sill following the vain beatings against the window panes to reach the freedom of the great outdoors. Perceive the absence of powdery scales— the ornamentation—of their wings. The peacock hibernates in more natural settings, such as hollow trees. If one is lucky, meaning favourable weather of course, this beauty can be seen on the wing as early as the first week of the month. It is a large butterfly and emits an audible 'clittering' from its wingbeat, similar to the hawker dragonflies.

The winter hot-spots for the bird watcher are reservoir, estuary and seaboard, and from November to February I devote much of my time there. Crouched behind the sea wall to escape the biting easterly wind, the estuarine scene pervades a timelessness that stirs the imagination.

The eye darts from the feeding waders at the water's edge to distant flighting duck high in the gin-clear sky, then back . . . And the twinkling water and soft, sit-up whee-oos from drake wigeon instil a precious serenity. Suddenly this calm is broken for an instant as a peregrine falcon hurtles into the already upward wheeling mass of evading dunlin and returns to the sand-bank opposite with a capture.

But estuary and coastal bird-spotting will soon fall from the birdwatcher's itineraries as the breeding season draws, to lands afar, the rich array of wader and duck that have wintered here. The spoonbill and little egret are now regular winter visitors and it is thrilling to muse on when and where these birds from the European mainland will begin to breed here in North Devon.

As natural habitat continues to recede apace gardens have become important sanctuaries for many bird species. Additionally, with the loss of many wooded areas, nest boxes placed in suitable areas of the garden have an important role to play to assist passerines such as titmice. This said, a few gardens' quotas of small birds will 'melt away'—not mine, though—as an increasing supply of insects and prospecting for natural nesting sites become an overpowering draw. The RSPB now says feed birds throughout the year—no harm done. More songbirds in towns and cities than in the country: a sad indictment of farming practice.

Why not whet the appetite for later in the year and draft a checklist of all the species that have appeared in the garden at one time or another. I have two lists, one for the more common appearances, the other for less likely sightings, just to get you started—good luck. To a degree the location of one's garden influences expected visitors—those fronting open countryside are likely to be at an advantage.

After an outside recording for a BBC Radio 4 programme based on my skylark anthology, my interviewer, a well-known naturalist and broadcaster, told me that during the previous summer a nightjar was actually resting on the roof of his garden shed. But then, he did live close to heathland.

I have heard locally of a sparrow hawk that hurtled in through the opening of a patio door, flew a circuit of the sitting-room in its pursuit of some small bird, then out again; this in a suburb of town. If posed the question, what species can we pencil in with integrity, I must answer all, however brief their stay. And no reason not to include swallow, house martin and swift, should any of these lovely birds nest in or on your property—or alight thereon.

A prolonged spell of snow or an iron-bound earth will usher in redwing, fieldfare and even skylark. And, mark well, the planting this spring of appropriate shrubs could in the future bring sustenance to a waxwing, siskin, or . . . . Although the majority of species are present during the period November to March a garden-bird checklist should not be considered the sole occupation of winter months. From time to time, in the region, rarities suddenly appear during the spring and summer months, so a high level of alertness should always be maintained (and remember to refill the birdbath daily with fresh water).

LIKELY VISITORS

wren	house sparrow	dunnock
blackbird	song thrush	greenfinch
chaffinch	starling	blue tit
coal tit	great tit	robin
pied wagtail	meadow pipit	marsh tit

POSSIBLE VISITORS

long-tailed tit	blackcap	goldcrest
garden warbler	chiffchaff	goldfinch
jackdaw	siskin	tree creeper
bullfinch	collared dove	nuthatch
fieldfare	black-headed gull	herring gull
wood pigeon	redwing	magpie
rook	linnet	great spotted woodpecker

The lists given above could be easily matched, or bettered, I dare say. Nonetheless, reeling off the names can project delightful imagery of particular birds and activities during visitations. And for that reason alone I think we should allow—should it deign to appear—even the predatory sparrow hawk on to the list.

The blackcap and chiffchaff are mainly spring and summer visitors, but during the last twenty-odd years many of their number have taken to over-wintering with us. The former finds nourishment on insects and berries, such as those produced by ivy and cotoneaster. In contrast the insectivorous chiffchaff must spend all its time searching out the tiny winged creatures on which to survive—apparently sewage farms are an ideal habitat during the harsh months as here a goodly supply of insects can still be found.

On its arrival at the end of April, the rather misleadingly named garden warbler could drop in and search the leaves of rose bushes, and similar foliage, for greenfly and other insects. This little bird actually frequents wooded habitats similar to those of the blackcap and, to the novice, its song is often confused with the latter species.

A spotted flycatcher is always a possibility in the larger garden. Grounds with mature conifers might even be visited by a firecrest. Herons have been known to inspect the fish-ponds of suburban tenants, who, rightly, become anxious, as nesting parents leave their home river to forage for their hungry young.

And, after two weeks of heavy rainfall that caused widespread flooding, a pair of kingfishers visited my small, raised, fish pond. The loss of several goldfish was, to my mind, more than compensated for by observing these gems among our birds, plunging into the water from the sprigs of honeysuckle trained to screen the garden shed.

Those places that have spacious grounds naturally have more chance of attracting some of the larger and less common garden birds. Once only have I been fortunate enough to observe the lesser spotted woodpecker close to human habitation. This was in the fruit and vegetable acreage which on the death, long since, of the cottage tenant, my paternal grandfather, was changed back to pasture-land. The transience of life!

And seen in the woodland encompassing a manor house, a pair of green woodpeckers. In yet another desirable residence I have counted five jays at one time at its farther reaches, but the lucky owner is also visited by green woodpeckers and nuthatches, greater spotted woodpeckers, and goldcrests feed regularly from the bird-table: this is quite apart from roe deer which banquet on his apples and rose bushes.

Magpies will occasionally trespass on to my current bird-table but to the previous garden there came but one—which I had omitted from previous lists because of its status. It could not be deemed to have been a naturally wild and free individual, but semi-tamed. A neighbour had reared it and while tending the garden or splitting logs for the hearth if would appear out of nowhere to alight on one's shoulder. It later became naturalized to the wild state, but I do wonder how long it survived the sights of a gun?

During the past fifty-odd years economic pressures have forced the bulk of the large country estates into becoming smaller and more viable units: the circumspect gamekeepers, who held sway over great tracts of the countryside, becoming a practically obsolete work force. However, their past activities are highlighted by those verminous crows and magpies that once hung on the gibbet alongside stoat, weasel and squirrel . . .

No longer persecuted to such a degree, and in strong numbers, are they making inroads into the population of the passerines? But let us not forget the fact that birds of prey, like sparrow hawk and buzzard, were also commonly installed on the gibbet—and the red kite population suffered a calamitous reduction in the late 18th/early 19th century from the attentions of the keepered shooting estates. However, the wheel has turned full circle and shooting estates are again a financial asset, and flourishing. But with new and enlightened management—and by legislation, let us not forget—flora and fauna are accorded sanctuary which would not be guaranteed if the land was put to conventional agricultural usage.

At close range, the sunlit plumage of the magpie reveals wonderfully unexpected green and blue iridescence . . . .

A pair of pied wagtails cavort beside the river.

For centuries local names for many of our wildflowers and birds were passed down orally from generation to generation. The first nature books often included the local/provincial names for each species alongside the generally recognised one. In 1910 W. Percival Westell did so in his *British Nesting Birds—a complete record of every species which nests in the British Isles*. These local, often very descriptive, names show how observant people were; one could say proportionately more so than the modern day as, then, their life's daily round closely interacted with the countryside about them.

Below is a list of birdnames once widely used in North Devon.

Robin	—Redocke, Ruddock
Mistle Thrush	—Holm Screech, Home Screech, Storm-Cock
Song Thrush	—Grey Drush, Trossel, Throstle, Thirstle
Blackbird	—Black Drush, Colly
Ring-Ouzel	—Moor-Blackbird, Rock-Ouzel, Tor-Ouzel
Wheatear	—Chickell
Redwing	—Windell, Windle, Winnel, Win'el, Windall, Winnard
Fieldfare	—Vole-Viers, Blue-Bird
Stonechat	—Furze (or "Fuzz") Chat
Whitethroat	—Whittybeard, White Drot, Nettle-creeper, Haysucker, Bee-bird
Goldcrest	—Tidley Goldfinch

Willow Warbler	—*Hay-bird, Ground Isaac, Ox-eye*
Hedge Sparrow	—*Dinnick, Segge*
Long-Tailed tit	—*Bottle-tit, Long-tailed Pie, Long-tailed Cap'n*
Great tit	—*Ackmeel, Ackmal, Ackmall, Ackmaul,*
	—*Hackmall, Heckmal, Hickmall, Hickemal,*
	—*Hickymal, Heckymal, Hackeymaul, Hagmall,*
	—*Big Hickmull, Eckmall, Uckmal, Ox-eye,*
	—*Black-headed Bob*
Blue tit	—*Billy-biter, Bluthpecker, Bluespick (N.D.),*
	Bluecap, Titmal, Ackmal: Dev.
Wren	—*Kitty Tope, Tidley Tope, Titty Todger,*
	Cracky or Crackil
Pied Wagtail	—*Dish-washer, Ditch-washer, Ditch-watcher,*
	Dishwash, Lady White Dishes
Spotted Flycatcher	—*Wall-plat*
Goldfinch	—*Gool finch, Blossom-Bird*
Chaffinch	—*Maze finch, Copper finch, White finch,*
	White winch, Silver Winch, Daffinch
Bullfinch	—*Hoop, Budfinch, Bud-picker, Coal-hood*
Yellow Hammer	—*Gladdy, Gladie, Gladdie, Golden Gladdy,*
	Yellow Yowley
Cirl Bunting	—*French Yellow Hammer*
Jay	—*Jay Pie*
Magpie	—*Pie, Mock-a-pie, Piannet*
Jackdaw	—*Daw, Chauk*
Hooded Crow	—*Mussel-crow*
Green Woodpecker	—*Woodwall, Woodawl, Woodwalf, Woodmaul,*
	Hoodall, Hoodwall, Oodall, Oodmall,
	Parrot Woodpecker
Cuckoo	—*Gowk, Gawk, Gookoo*
Buzzard	—*Kit, Kitt, Keet, Kite, Black Kite*
Kestrel—	—*Windfanner, Windhover, Criss Hawk,*
	Crasset Hawk
Gannet	—*Channel goose*
White-fronted Goose	—*Laughing Goose*
Shelduck	—*Burrow Duck*
Pintail	—*Pheasant Duck, Sea-pheasant*
Red-breasted Merganser	—*Spike-billed Wigeon*
Wood-pigeon	--- *Culver*
Stock-Dove	— *Culver*
Black Grouse	—*Moor Blackbird, Heath Poult*
Water Rail	—*Skiddy Cock, Skit-y-cock, Skip Cock,*
	Skitty Cock, grey Skit, Gutter cock, Ore cock
Lapwing	—*Peewit, Lapwink, Horniwink,*
	Northam Hornywink

Woodcock	—*Muff-cock*
Jack Snipe	—*Jack, Half snipe, Atterflitter*
Dunlin	—*Purre, Sea Lark, Summer Lark*
Redshank	—*Pill-cock*
Bar-tailed Godwit	—*Sea Woodcock, Goddin*
Whimbrel	—*Half Curlew, Jack Curlew*
Red-throated Diver	—*Herring-Bone, Sprat Loon, Loon*
Little Grebe	—*Dipchick*
Puffin	—*Lundy Parrot, Coulter-neb, Nath, Pope*
Manx Shearwater	—*Cuckle or Cockle*

Mud-paste images of their creators, innumerable worm casts rise from the rain-sodden ground. Is there a more beneficial organism to the soil than the worm (apart from companion bacteria) and, therefore, ultimately our welfare? Do we care?

Daylight appreciably lengthens as the stage of the month advances.

At the month's end new shoots of cow parsley push up around the dead but stalwart flower stalks that have remained aloft a full two seasons. In the lane the periwinkle opens its blue flowers at the hedge top where the hazel boughs are festooned with pollened catkins. At the side of the lane numerous spear-headed leaves of ramsons have pierced through the soil, appended here and there with gloss-green, ink-blotted leaves of wild arum. In a similar position but also claiming half the depth of the hedgebank dogs mercury begins its annual carpeting growth. Signs aplenty that the sap is rising.

At the fresh and serene haunts of woodland border, river-bank, streamside and hedgebank the wild daffodils begin to appear—soon to open and sparkle at the sun's touch: always a time for the countryside connoisseur to savour.

THE DAFFODIL

For oft, when on my couch I lie
In vacant or in pensive mood,
They flash upon that inward eye
Which is the bliss of solitude:
And then my heart with pleasure fills,
And dances with the daffodils.

Wordsworth

SPRING

From the stark beauty of nature held in limbo we have moved, imperceptibly, to fresh, exuberant spring . . .

The warming earth pushes forth floral heralds of forthcoming splendour; each annual return seems more glorious yet more precious than the last. With wonderful and boundless marvels, preoccupied nature enriches all those who approach her altar. Implicit feelings attach to each passing day.

It is an eternal realisation that enraptures the soul.

The meek snowdrop bows out winter and leads in the season of growth and nature's finest hour. Daffodils and primroses follow on, rearing their defiant elegance along hedgerow, woodland border and riverbank. The yellow, trumpet-headed daffodils sway as one to the yet uncloistered breeze and offer a hint of fragrance therewith. Primroses, from which 'placidity itself surely derived', stud the ground with softest yellow. Later these plants become engulfed by the re-emerging bracken, or intermingle with the woodland bluebells that spread a deep-blue coverlet in every shadowy dell.

The land is charged with impending vitality,
procreation the *raison d'être* of all its glories.

The interlaced world of nature announces itself on its very emergence. The wave of animation will lap every plant, stone and fissure: myriads of *minutiae* create the natural resurgence.

What words could do justice to these rich times? The great body of human society has cocooned itself from the world of nature. Thus detached, we have become desensitized to its many glories. Spring is a time of pure joy, when hill and vale resound to tunes from joyous songbirds.

> I heard a thousand blended notes,
> While in a grove I sate reclined.

(from 'In Early Spring' – *Wordsworth*)

From the maroon flush of the terminal bud scales on the woodland crown the deft strokes of springtime are soon manifold. The bare-limbed trees and understorey bushes are gradually cloaked with leaves which have burst free and unfurl into the sweet and warming air. The shades of living green cannot be replicated.

> I was for that time lifted above earth;
> And possest joys not promis'd in my birth.

(from 'The Compleat Angler'   *Izaak Walton*)

Bluebells, wood-sorrel and wood anemone fill the hazel-grove with colour. It is a crime to wander from the path for each stride would, even with the greatest care, deal a crushing blow to some tender plant. Along the hedgebanks and elsewhere the red campion reappears in number, and in woodland and lane the air is redolent with the pungent scent of ramsons or wild garlic.

An early flowering member of the carrot family Alexanders—so named because it originates from Macedonia, the country of Alexander the Great—is also recognised for its smell. Its rank growth along the base of hedgerows and in ditches and the greenish yellow flowers supported from long stalks, are a flora hallmark of mid to late spring. Its *Umbelliferae* relations, cow parsley and hogweed, are advancing their distinctive contrasting leaf growth through much of Alexanders domination, but both will have a similar impact before long. Indeed, the white or pink flushed umbels of hogweed are present from late spring through to autumn, a boon for many insects.

Miraculously, spring reels back the creatures not endemic to this latitude. The classic example is undoubtedly the swallow, returning to last year's haunts after traversing awesome expanses of desert, land and sea. The petite warblers are also back, to charm the eye and ear.

> "Chiff-chaff, chiff-chaff!" The double note rang triumphantly. The yellowish scrap of feathers had crossed all Europe from the south to reach this same Welsh valley again. The wonder of it in me was a boy's wonder that would never die out of the heart of the man. It humbled me once more, as knowledge of the eternal in nature does.
>
> (from 'The Golden Year' – *R.M. Locksley*)

Sand martins again circle over the rivers: the call of the cuckoo is a tease to the listener and centuries' long rural history seems condensed into 'cuckoo, cuckoo'. Swifts, scythers of the air, put in a late spring appearance. Headlands become the landfall for many a migrant; on one I have seen a number of whitethroats—resting up before dispersing deep into the vibrant countryside. Also slipping in comes the spotted fly-catcher, quiet in tone, quiet in habit—and quietly loved . . .

> the wonder of it in me . . .

Insubstantial butterflies, moths, dragonflies and other insects achieve unimaginable distances to reach our shores. More in fable than in fact, the painted lady butterfly is reported as sometimes arriving in numbers so dense as to resemble a cloud. What a spectacle—and all from a starting point in North Africa.

The red admiral butterfly also travels back from this same continent, and from southern Spain, to create new broods, many of which will return south in the autumn. Some will become prominent visitors to our gardens, sipping most decoratively at the over-ripe apples, plums and raspberries left by the attentive birds—and by owners who are in sympathy with nature.

On leaving the Sargasso sea boot-lace sized and transparent elvers—young eels—have, during three years of eastward drifting, navigated the vastness of the Atlantic ocean to reach our estuarine waters. Here their journey impels them to battle against the river-flow to reach the streams and ditches of the hinterland. A prodigious feat, repeated through aeons, generation upon generation.

Fired with conflicting purpose, the mad March hare races hither and thence about the sunny grass slope, to do battle with any rival male, a jack, and to be an attentive show-off, with fancy for the discerning female.

In the bird kingdom throughout the extending daylight hours activity is unceasing. There is song and display, pairing up, and nidification. First, building material must be sought and ferried to the nest site: then the laying and incubation of clutches of eggs and, on the hatching of the delicate, pastel coloured eggs, the feeding of young. An endless supply of nourishment has to be obtained, and sustained for a period of weeks—be it insects or seeds,—for the ever ravenous brood.

Lapwings in display flights are now seen almost daily: great and lesser spotted woodpeckers 'drumming'; green woodpecker 'laughing'; woodcock 'drumming'; snipe 'whiffling'.

Paired curlews head for the high ground of marsh and moor, to nesting sites of old. With nests and broods secreted in hedgerow, tree and ivied wall the song thrush, blackbird, robin, wren, chaffinch and dunnock become attentive parents, but, giving vent to the mood of these ambrosial days, steal time to sing with vigour.

And always, the insuppressible skylarks and a rain of melody.

> For it (skylark) inspired a bard to win
> Ecstatic heights in thought and rhyme.
>
> *Thomas Hardy*

With each fresh shower, plant growth quickens, to face the synthesising sun.

THE ALL-PERVASIVE APPEAL IS KEENLY FELT

MARCH

Awake, awake, for the springtime's sake,
  March daffodils too long dreaming,
The lark is high in the spacious sky
  And the celandine's stars are gleaming.
The gorse is ablaze, and the woodland sprays
  Are purple as August heather
The buds unfurl, and the mavis and merle
  Are singing duets together.

he inner feeling of optimism that spring is on its way is now supported by the evidence—if one but looks for it.

Rooks, tending newly laid clutches of pale greenish eggs, blotched with brown, are among the first to avail themselves of nature's gradual departure from winter's trial. The heronry has also been in active service for some weeks now and the forthcoming hatchlings will replace the wintertime casualties and augment the colony.

Rookeries are the embodiment of rurality.

Surely a village without a rookery is a village found wanting. Throughout living memory there has been a rookery in the centre of my home village. Standing close to the eastern perimeter wall of the graveyard, adjacent to the church and its most impressive tower overlooking the square, the hulking Scots pine contains many nests on its sturdy boughs. Twigs cemented at the base with mud, and a lining of grass, wool and hair, make solid yet snug homes for the annual broods.

Due to a population surge, space on the tree has been exhausted and some of the younger generation have, by necessity, had to establish a new nesting colony at the Vicarage—lying a mile due east of the church. Here in the spacious grounds the conifers and elms provide ideal quarters. Our sacrosanct rooks.

Rookeries are normally established in the crown of the tallest trees in a particular neighbourhood. In some areas this provides maximum distance from disapproving farmers and landowners, who annually attempt to blast away nests and contents with twelve-bore shot-guns. By far and away the most impregnable rookery I know is the one occupying the avenue of Chile pines—perhaps better known as monkey puzzles—on a local National Trust estate.

From an acceptable distance to its inhabitants the rookery can hold the attention of the observer for lengthy periods. There is perpetual motion: the constant activity and noise have an almost hypnotic effect. The feeble—and not so feeble—pleading cries of nestlings are suddenly strangled as food, regurgitated by parent birds from their throat pouches under the tongue, plops into ever demanding red gapes. With another feeding mission accomplished the adults proceed to wipe clean their bills on a twig close by their respective nests before flying back to adjacent fields. You should listen out for the cawing notes of a sitting or incoming rook: occasionally they lower in tone to become almost a growl.

The carrion crow is, by habit, the antithesis of cousin rook and although its nest is built in a similar fashion a colony bird it most definitely is not. A distance of a mile or more between nesting pairs is the norm. The carrion crow's nest is also far more accessible, being positioned in a tree that is often a climbable hedgebank oak. Many countrymen must hold the memory of how, during their youth, this corvid provided the first opportunity of real adventure by climbing up and examining a wool-lined nest and its clutch of eggs or brood of young.

Another corvid in the area is the 'imperial' raven. I know of three nesting pairs, two of which are in the tops of pine trees, the first in a tree at the top of a plantation. The second is in one of a huddle of pines growing on the crown of a steep field overlooking the river valley. Here the breeding pair have been established for over fifty years and (apart from the ever-lessening menace from egg collectors) I can see no reason why they should move elsewhere, for the landowner is a model of tradition and thankfully tree-felling is all but a natural process. The third nesting site is on the coastline, on a rock ledge. Here again the pair have been long established, the one threat possibly posed by peregrine falcons which are not averse to requisitioning the bulky home of a fellow frequenter of these inhospitable cliff-sides.

I have watched a raven gorging on carrion on a narrow pebble beach, then fly to the cliff-top to disgorge the meal and proceed, with surprising daintiness (considering its thick heavy bill) to savour the relaid feast. These masterly birds of flight revel in high winds, tumbling and rolling and uttering harsh croaks that can only be signalling sheer enjoyment.

With spring's arrival curlews return to breed on the high ground of moorland and marsh. Bringing a special magic to the water meadow in an area a short distance to the northeast of the village, a pair of curlews are an annual treat. Typically the water (or plash) meadow bears areas of floating mosses marked with rushes. And cuckoo flower, or lady's smock, those lilac/silver white flowers we, as children, referred to as "milk maids" grow liberally here during late spring and early summer.

Standing in the middle of the meadow are two splendid, symmetrical oaks, one being the annual nesting quarter for a pair of carrion crows. The pair guard the territory zealously, and I have seen them harry away the inward flying pair of innocent curlews on more than one occasion. But the curlews, I'm glad to say, are not long deterred from such a pleasant abode—and neither should they be.

In this selfsame meadow I have also seen hares but, as with the curlews, I have made no attempt at finding form or nest, being of a mind to permit no nuisance to their brood-rearing. To my thinking, the curlew's 'bubbling song', together with the year round "cur-lee", is a distillation of, and evocation to, the very atmosphere of its open and often lonely haunts: as is the plaintive cry of the lapwing or 'peewit' . . .

Heart-stirring sounds to the watcher of the wild.

March bids *au revoir* to most of the wintering birds who forsake our warming shores. The countryside seems, at least for a short while, deserted, bereft of the pleasing flocks of redwings, fieldfares, finches and other migrants that have bolstered the numbers of our own species. But the lull is only temporary; happily, summer immigrants will soon be arriving.

Before the month is out, ringing from the still scant hedgerow will come the soft "chiff-chaff, chiff-chaff" call of the pioneer warbler. For many days a cock chaffinch has been declaiming a strident rendition of 'hoo-eet' to tease me into the belief that I am hearing my first willow warbler of the year. However, I know I shall have to wait a few more weeks before the arrival, from tropical West Africa—a journey of some 3,000 miles—of this, the second of the much-loved leaf-warbler trio.

The first of the *hirundines*, sand martins, arrive—around the third week of the month—in colony-sized flocks, wheeling and arcing high over the river, trawling the air for the few winged insects as are abroad at this point of the new season. Wheatears, freshly arrived, are understandably lacking in their normal vigour, but on resting up will soon recapture all the dynamism that is associated with these birds of our open areas.

On moorland and common the last of the year's swayling is complete, the smoke-smell lingering for days after the controlled firing has been extinguished. (How different is the picture when a summertime drought and human carelessness spells disaster for nesting birds and numerous types of wildlife such as snakes, lizards, plants and insects.) Within a couple of weeks new shoots will regenerate the dun-patched, fire-blackened slopes, and the wheel of life revolve afresh.

The winter-long accumulation of cow-dunged straw-bedding from the cattle sheds is now being spread on the fields: an open invitation for the rooks to move in and rummage for insects and the odd ear of corn.

In the grass fields farmers are out perforce with tractor-drawn iron or stone rollers. In the days of my youth hayfields were a common, though relished, summertime scene with a single harvest—in June or July—largely without detriment to ground-nesting birds. In fact the mixed grasses and wildflowers drew vast numbers of insects and was a sanctuary for all manner of other animals. Cutting the binding cord of a bale of hay releases the essence of summer past, for there is 'sunlight in the smell'.

Sadly, hayfields are as rare today as corncrakes. Silaging is now the common practice, and the multiple-cropped fields of Italian rye grass have turned the countryside into patchwork zones of desert, unsupportive to, and devoid of, wildlife, a condition further exacerbated by the more recent introduction of maize-tilling for winter cattle feed—necessitating treatment by problematic herbicides.

The indexing of daytime bisects upwards creeping temperatures with expanding light. Along banks and hedgerows, synchronising with the sandmartins' arrival, wall speedwell and goosegrass appear. On the Burrows thyme-leafed speedwell has flowered—it's ahead of its time: my pocket guide gives April. Well in excess of four hundred plant species have been recorded here—the paradisian Burrows.

In the dune slacks, the silky, hairy twigs of creeping willow and, in the carr, the silver-coated buds holding the embryonic leaves of sallow or 'pussy willow' are beginning to receive inquiring visits from the queen bumble bees, *Bombus terrestris*. With thrumming flight these over-wintered insects frequently break from the reconnoitre of the branches and dip right down to ground level, scouring for a suitable orifice, either excavated by small mammals or rent by the subterranean root systems of the salix. This investigation is in order to establish, single handed, the later bustling underground colonies.

Sea buckthorn is now flowering, though this event is easily overlooked owing to the smallness of the green petal-less structures. (It is classed as dioecious, which means that male and female flowers are on separate plants.) In recent years this thicket-forming small tree has become established on the opposite side of the estuary from the Burrows and this I attribute to the birds that have fed on the berry-laden bushes of autumn and who afterwards flew there.

The lichen-covered gate leading into the woodland has dammed the windswept leaves of autumn and winter. Here the deeply layered beech leaves are host to a number of wolf spiders, lying motionless over the ochre surface. Poised to snatch some luckless fly unawares, their senses detect footfall: one is conscious of barely detectable movement as multiple black forms nimbly shoot into the crevices proffered by the light settlement of the leaves.

Slowly but surely, as sunny days draw them, the smaller creatures come out of hiding. Wolf spiders, sometimes in groups up to ten or more strong, are suddenly back on dry wall and bank, each one intent on catching an insect prey by a 'blink of the eye' leap, followed by a stab of their poisonous fangs. At this significantly early stage, when, through fewness, things abroad are quickly noted: the crab spider is also homed-in and closely inspected. Spiders, of the order *Araneae*, class arachnids, provide us with compelling study. Likewise insects, of twenty five main divisions, in the class *Insecta* :

'numerous as the sands which bend the seas'

Rupert Brooke

The first minute insect larvae begin to feast off the freshest of foliage. Caterpillars of certain lepidoptera arise from hibernation to crop the food-plant of their choice. And the intrepid ants reconnoitre old haunts . . .

Over the rich, yellow face of the gorse, bee-like in habit and number, seven-spot ladybirds whirl in wide arcs, surveying the thorny crowns for an unattached mate. On closer examination the threatening spines hold any number of these attractive beetles, almost all of them coupled.

Assuming that the small tortoiseshell and peacock butterflies have been encountered already this year, this is the month to add two or more names to the list. The two new arrivals I have in mind are the brimstone and the speckled wood. The first is a beauty, and one's heart often skips a beat each new year when it is first sighted, sailing majestically along over sun-touched hedgerows and woodland borders. My earliest record for this species is 8th February.

By contrast the speckled wood has a singular preference for shadier habitats, flying in short bursts and then resting. One may also be rewarded with the sighting of a comma butterfly, perhaps as when it has alighted on foliage or the ground at the edge of woodland. In such a place, under an overhanging hazel bough, I have watched this fine species, dressed in deep tawny red, and with unique, ragged-contoured wings, dabbing its proboscis to imbibe moisture from a patch of bare earth. To me these beautiful insects, with such tenuous hold on life, never fail to elicit wonder and joy.

As plant growth quickens, further butterflies and insects will be appearing in the finest livery.

Moths to the lighted window: I can testify that, yes indeed, the oak beauty is a beautiful moth as I have examined close-up an individual which is resting on the outside of my door having been attracted to the light from my porch.

Moths disturbed along woodland pathsides.

On a warm, windless day a swarm of gnats may be seen, and one or two individuals always seem to find their way into the house: long-legged hump-backed insects, very similar in shape and size to a species of crane-fly that comes out in the autumn. The 'blood-worms' of the midges—that are also prone to swarming—may be found in any stagnant pool of water.

Found under wood debris, with a slim spiral shell, is the plaited door snail. Butterbur is coming into flower, brightening several broad roadside verges in the district: it is months in advance of the habitat-sharing, and similarly noticeable species, the common comfrey with its 'stands'. In the hedge above one such butterbur stronghold, the elderberry is breaking out in leaf, one of the earliest of the larger plants so to do.

Like sacs of dew leaflets of elm hang on the 'ribs' of hedgerows. From the moment of opening—nascence—these are coarse to the touch.

The greening over of the countryside, by grasses and other plants, daily becomes more perceptible. Nettle patches shoot up with a flourish of aromatic freshness. Docks re-appear, usually where least desired. The new light-green shoots on the brambles are easily distinguished from the growth of previous years.

Opposite-leafed golden saxifrage forms soft, yellow-green mats on a hedgebank and at the side of a woodland stream. Moschatel, which appears as a larger version of saxifrage, occurs where this stream emerges into the field. It can be easily overlooked owing to its inconspicuous greenish flowers—with four 'faces' it is also known as the 'town hall clock'.

A few dandelions flaunt their golden splendour, attracting the attention of early rising honey and bumble bees. Along the edges of river and stream alike the white flowers of the crowfoot bloom.

One's wildflower list for the opening months makes a sudden spurt for, on the tail-coats of March, a number of species appear to supplement the regular daffodil, periwinkle, primrose, celandine, scurvy grass (in some districts) opposite-leaved golden-saxifrage, march marigold—or kingcup—crowfoot and a smattering of dandelion and daisy. Three-cornered leek, common dog violet, wild strawberry, dogs mercury and bittercress extend the list. And along many country roadsides and wooded areas wood spurge is the commonest of the late March into late spring plants. Very soon there will be ribwort plantain, timothy grass and field wood-rush . . .

On my return I dwell on two faithful signposts to nature's forthcoming treasury: the tell-tale rustling of movement over dry foliage, where a timorous lizard has not trusted to its excellent protective colouration and has scuttled into hiding .... and from the still scanty foliage of the hedgerow, the beckoning "chiff-chaff, chiff-chaff, chiff-chaff" ringing notes of the pioneer warbler.

30th. One swallow appears over the village.

WITH EXPECTATION RIFE, THE COUNTRYSIDE IS AN IRRESISTIBLE LURE.

APRIL

A RICH AND FULL MONTH INDEED.

The nature-diarist should not be wanting of sub-ject-matter as recordings are all but constant . . .
3rd. The odd bluebell opening.
Calendar months are not physical barriers in the lives of flora and fauna, and although many species are associated with certain times of the year, there is an inevitable overlapping. Many of the wildflowers and insects of Maytime are sparingly represented before April is out—our reunion with them unfailingly sweet.

Oh, the lovely fickleness of an April day.

'Pastoral Days' – *W. H. Gibson*

With fluctuating conditions, sunshine to shower, both sunny and oft chill, April is fickle right enough yet is also an irrefutable confirmation of springtime. The trickle of fresh life will, in a few short weeks, quickly burgeon to a torrent in rai-ment of green. And if, as diarists, at April's outset we feel a certain confidence in the undertaking of listing all new appearances, be assured at her close we shall feel daunted, yet jubilant, by nature's fecund store . . .

Lesser celandine is now at its glorious best, and on a sunny day hedgebanks and meadows are daubed with burnished gold.

There is a flower, the lesser Celandine
That shrinks, like many more, from cold and rain
And, the first moment that the sun may shine
Bright as the sun himself, 'tis out again.

William Wordsworth

We cheat our senses to simply award a cursory look at even the commonest wildflower for each is a wonder of nature's construction.

Appreciate this wonder: observe afresh and with tender care the colour, architecture and science of each and every plant species as an ever increasing number of these beauties reach inflorescence. Characteristic of their chosen habitat of cultivated ground are lilac-coloured ivy-leaved toadflax, germander speedwell (commonly known as birdseye) and hairy bittercress. Common fumitory (fumitory—from the Latin 'smoke of the earth') also affects bare patches of cultivated or disturbed ground and has eye-catching pink, with darker-tipped petalled flowers. It is an unmistakable, sprawling, vetch-like plant and, although it looks and sometimes rises like one, it does not possess the tendrils of the true climber.

The dandelion, predominantly a grassland plant, will soon challenge the celandine with yellow wash. Daisies will be prolific by month's end—galaxies reflected on fields. Wild strawberry, and dog and sweet violet appear, mainly on hedgerows and woodland borders, the dog violet also appearing along coastal and railway tracks and the like.

This is an important plant (not least for its peculiar attractiveness)—it is the larval food-plant for most of the impressive fritillary butterfly tribe and, after hibernating through the long winter months, caterpillars of some of the species will now be feeding on its leaves. Along the fringes of pond, stream and river the upright leaves of yellow flag, or iris, eventually to stand tall, commence their growth.

Year on year, Alexanders seems to extend its range along the local hedgerows near sea-level. Inspected closely the plant surprises with its structure, from the green and yellow umbels to the sheath-like lined leaf stalks butting under the flower stems. It is supplying nourishment to many

Microdiptera and other small insects, the precursors of the later army.

In field and hedgeside docks and nettles, the food-plants of many of our butterflies, arise. The common scurvy-grass is now not only a feature of the saltmarsh and tidal riverbank, but also thrives along hedgerows far inland—at an altitude that is at odds with its normal marine habitat—its extensive colonization transforming these sites into botanical snow-drifts.

The plentiful white flowers of the greater stitchwort star the hedgerows: later, their swollen seed-heads will be a source of amusement to children who, pinching them between finger and thumb, achieve a satisfying 'pop'.

Also to be found are garlic mustard, or 'Jack-by-the-hedge' (the food-plant of the larva of the exquisite orange-tip butter-fly), the early purple orchid and the wild arum—known also as cuckoo-pint, lords and ladies, or parson's in the pulpit.

In a handful of noted hedgebank sites, Dame's Violet *Hesperis matronalis* reliably reappears. Cow parsley, which pushed up its ferny leaves on purplish stalks the preceding month, is coming to the fore, its white umbels attracting a steadily increasing number of insects along the hedgerows, ditches and roadsides.

Within the month on so-called 'waste-land' (where nature, for a time, is allowed free rein) the patch containing the love-ly coltsfoot has seen its flowers followed by the 'clocks'. The heart-shaped leaves do not appear until flowering has taken place.

Goat willow, or sallow, is in these parts a prominent spring-time bush or tree. Of separate sex, the catkins of the male plants are thick-coated with yellow pollen (bumble bees extract a rich harvest from these), female catkins are a bare green.

Dog's mercury now forms its familiar patches even into the woodland depths as well as at its edges and the lower sections of the hedgerow borders, leading to sun-dappled fields. Also present here is another family member, the sun spurge, a plant that when children we labelled 'snake's food'—well, it is poisonous, is that the link?

The unmistakable yellow archangel (close cousin of dead-nettle and hempnettle) is beginning to flower in long estab-lished patches of woodland and wooded borders. Some of the upper leaves, normally a deep green, quite often show exten-sive light blotches and streaks.

So many of our popular wildflower names originate from folklore of each district, when they provided an important and much needed benefit as a herbalists' cure. Sour-gap was another childhood label, used this time for the wood sorrel, the leaves of which we picked and ate. Only recently did I read that this plant contains oxalic acid, injurious to heart and kidneys—hence its Latin name *Oxalis acetosella*. Although normally a dweller of woodland and its shady environment, this lovely, delicate, white-flowering plant can also be found hereabouts on hedgebanks, the flowers markedly suffused with purple.

Garden weeds become prevalent if left to their own devices, with water horsetail being the crowning glory. This plant is a veritable back-breaker and spirit-dampener to workers of ground with a high water table, e.g. lying alongside stream, river or marsh. The rootstems penetrate downwards two feet or more, making total eradication virtually impossible. In spring, the stalks (containing spore) appear like miniature pine forests. During prehistory these plants grew as tall as trees in the first swamp-forests, inhabited by dragonflies with prodigious wingspans, said to exceed 2 feet (60 cm).

There are many notable garden 'weeds': broad-leaved wil-low herb, red dead-nettle, dandelion, shepherd's purse, ground ivy, germander speedwell or bird's eye, chickweed and groundsel are some of them. Most of these flower at intervals throughout the year and are really attractive plants in their own right, if one can suppress one's bias as a gardener.

In the early times of their long reign on earth, millions of years before the evolution (let alone the ascent) of man, plants, which were then single-sexed, produced pollen for cross-pollination and fertility: the pollen had to be borne on the wind to achieve this however. But later, with the highly successful development and radiation of insect species, plants tapped this resource by forming, over aeons, a new dynamic reproductive structure out of their leaves—flowers!

The petals of this new creation encircled both the stamens (male organs) and styles (female organs)—a far less wasteful means of regeneration was under way. Of course not all species choose the same path. Dogs mercury for example, a plant of ancient lineage, does not bear flowers in the recognised sense—to achieve pollination the petal-less tassels of the single-sexed plants release pollen to the breezes, and some of the multitudinous fine grains will, sooner or later, lodge on the upright tassels of the opposite gender.

Stinging nettles likewise produce pollen, the male plants having developed catkins which burst open to shower the styles of adjacent female plants. Conifers aside, being of the most ancient lineage, some trees pollinate in a similar manner to nettles, and bear pollened catkins that are a hallmark of early spring. Normally the catkins are of male gender only but if the tree is of the dual-sexed kind the female flowers sit close by, more often than not overlooked by the walker. (The sallow bears catkins of both sexes, but on separate trees.)

The hazel is a good example of holding both sexes, the male catkins releasing pollen grains before the female budlike flowers are open, thereby preventing self-pollination and the possible weakening of heredity allied to this. By producing blossom ahead of its leaves the blackthorn steals a march on the hawthorn. Its showy, delicate white blooms attract, like Alexanders, large numbers of insects, mainly of the *Diptera* order, but towards the end of the month bee and insect banqueting passerines such as chiffchaffs and other perching birds are frequently in attendance about the crown.

The ash tree produces flower clusters of purplish-red before the black buds burst open to release the tender leaves. Both alder and oak now bear anthers; the beech holds blossom.

A small totally black humble bee visits the garden.

The handsome grey wagtail gives a sharp 'te-seep' as it leaves one rocky boulder for another further down-stream. It dips and dabs there with characteristic wagtail movements. The nest is built in a hole in a riverbank, sometimes concealed by undergrowth cascading from the top. The yellow wagtail is a spring and summer visitor, preferring a far less watery abode for its stay—a lovely species. The pied wagtail is much commoner than its cousins and will by now be nesting in dry stone walls and stream banks.

Throughout the year the pied wagtails are quiet birds, until now: the males of the kind are suddenly charged with a combativeness which manifests itself in a sparring match with their own reflections in the window panes of sheds or main buildings. And quite prolonged are these 'fights'.

Spring and summer visiting birds arrive from winter retreats. Sand martins, insectivores through and through, skim to and fro above the surface of the river, twittering excitedly as they feed on the tiny winged insects that congregate there. The house martin, although a close cousin of the former, does not enjoy the same haunts; it prefers close proximity to man's habitation, where the domed mud nest is attached to the eaves of farm buildings, or of houses of both town and country. The ringing of house martins and swallows has proved conclusively that they return to the same locations each year.

Swallows return around Easter-time, immediately swooping across the fields with their own rapturous spirit and bringing always a rapture to every following eye; one swallow's appearance may not make a summer, but it maketh this man inwardly rejoiceful.

A willow warbler, just arrived from tropical West Africa, plucks insects from the catkins and is dusted with pollen to match its own soft colouring. The 'fluff' of the sallow catkins is used to line the nests of birds. Altogether the sallow is a valuable resource of fauna, particularly in springtime.

The plaintive "too-eet, too-eet" of the willow-warbler now matches for regularity the chiffchaff's call along the spring hedgerows. The third party of the affectionately titled 'leaf warblers' is the slightly larger and eye-catching wood warbler, bearer of yellow patches above the eye, on the throat and side of neck. It is a woodland bird, and the unusual 'two-songs' contrast from the canopy is relished. And with 'bins', that necklaced appendage, one can enter the magical upper tree world where the shiver song is performed. It is a bird that stops and engrosses the watcher; a little early yet perhaps, but just wait till May when the woodlands will resound with wood warbler voices.

Two further members of the warbler family (*Sylviidae*) are the blackcap and whitethroat, both captivating subjects to the quiet watcher. The blackcap is the most secretive of the two, preferring the quiet of shaded brushy areas of woodland and the like, while by contrast, the whitethroat is a lover of leafy hedgerows, where, on being disturbed, it utters an agitated "churr, churr".

Somewhere about the hawthorn comes a repeated 'zwee, zoowee, zwee, zwee'. The rendition is terminated with a hurried 'chirrup' as the bird takes wing—a cock greenfinch: resplendent in breeding-season attire. Towards the end of the month I have observed the group courtship of greenfinches. Twelve or so birds, cocks outnumbering the few hens, were all perched in a single tree, a hawthorn. With attention-seeking wing-droops and flicks the cock greenfinches courted their demure opposites. In the warming mid-morn sunshine, and putting aside their main activity to onlook this exhibition, are a dunnock or two, a hen blackbird, a robin and blackcap.

The lapwing flock, having long concluded the impressive aerial displays that are a feature of their courtship, settle into the task of chick raising. In the district, lapwings have nested in the same field for several seasons, being thankfully free of interference from farm machinery or nest robbers; a gratifying situation since most ground nesting birds (the corncrake being the classic example) can fall foul to a host of dangers in addition to these.

(Land drainage puts an end to whole communities of life—an ecosystem rich and increasingly rare, of plants, insects and birds—and continues apace: even though during days of heavy downpour the now concentrated and uncontainable volumes of water sweep away to the river-valleys countless tons of fertile soil).

Altogether the lapwing is a charming bird, calls of 'peewit' as dear to me as to every watcher of the wild. Its iridescent plumes make it a graceful subject one never tires of watching, and its crest is a unique feature among British birds (forgetting the skylark—the hoopoe cannot be considered, being a bird of passage and enjoyed by only a handful of fortunate people each year).

By and large, the resident birds have already hatched the first clutches of delicately patterned eggs. The nests in which these are contained are far more endearing than mere receptacles, in many cases being works of intricate and delicate skill focused through that singular tool, the bill. Plus, of course, hour upon hour of patient industry.

Favourites for the honour of master craftsman must surely be chaffinch and long tailed tit. The flawless cup-shaped nest of the chaffinch is woven from wool, moss and lichen and snugly lined with feathers and cattle hair. I always delight in their discovery: of four nests found in one season, three were in the forked branches of apple trees, a favourite site as here lichens are readily available. Once found adjoining every farmyard, the apple orchards of my youth are but a memory, a very sad reflection in every sense of the word. Governments encourage and dissuade with equal potency: grants made years earlier for the planting of orchards were in the 1960s reversed to finance their destruction, and the generations-old culture built around the apple became another victim scattered beside the roadway to efficiency.

The long-tailed tit weaves an oval-shaped domed nest of lichen, cobwebs and cattle hair and this is lined with countless small feathers—as many as two thousand. The structure is elastic and this allows room for the growing brood of between 8 to 12 nestlings. A crooked tail denotes a recent spell of incubation on the part of a (usually female) parent. It has been noted that adults other than the parents will participate in feeding the youngsters, perhaps single birds or pairs that have been unsuccessful in their own attempts at brood raising. Predators such as sparrow hawks are no respecters of the nesting season, having their own broods demanding to be fed . . .

Once, on one of those quasi-birdnesting jaunts (when nests are visited, but in no way molested), I heard considerable 'bird fuss' emanating from the hedge in the top corner of the steeply-sloped coppiced wood through which I was threading my way. Edging forward, I found that the alarm calls were being uttered by a pair of blackbirds, scolding with all their might a pair of leering magpies that compounded the scene with their own retort. But the blackbirds' vigorous defence seemed only to encourage the robbers, who, while I could only look on, destroyed the whole clutch of eggs. Should I have intervened? With hindsight probably yes, but what would then have transpired? Surely, although foiled by human intervention on one occasion, a further raid could be envisaged from such opportunists.

An interesting entry of mine, dating back to the spring of 1966, revealed the discovery of four nests, all sited within 20 paces' length of hedgerow.

Bird prescience in the nesting season! A few weeks ago I watched incredulously as the mistle thrushes began nest construction in the exposed forked boughs of the hazel—the work not totally hidden by the advancing tendrils of ivy. And goldfinches, building in the bare beech hedge—likewise 'thoughtless'. Until, shortly after, bud cases released fresh leaves to hide the respective nurseries. Both pairs of birds were successful in raising their broods . . .

Standing on the rim of their bulky twig nursery two fully-fledged ravens are exercising their wings . . .

Within comfortable walking distance from my home village I found three nesting colonies of jackdaws. The nearest is on the ledges of an old quarry, where something like ten pairs nest annually, amidst an atmosphere of noisy bickering. The second colony occupies the ledge of the iron girders which support the railway over the river; here, five or six pairs are established. The final site is in the chimney stacks of a long since fire-gutted building—at the last inspection the home of two nesting pairs. (In my new village jackdaws nest in the bell-tower, preferring to stay outside during bell-ringing times. Pity the poor youngsters!)

These mischievous birds are unscrupulous in their eagerness to set up home, and many a house-owner has found to his chagrin that his chimney has become unusable, being solidly sealed with twigs and wool. Pet jackdaws are notorious for their kleptomania, and I can still recall the antics of a 'daw' reared in the village where I attended primary school. One day at playtime the bird flew down, snatched the handkerchief from my hand and deposited it high up in the oak tree overlooking the playground. It was in this same playground that I came across my one and only death's head hawk moth which I found lying on the tarmacadam, a startling introduction to the sphingidae!

Walking up through the grass margin between the fir plantation and roadside hedge, I once disturbed a hen common partridge and her brood of chicks. She flew off and the chicks skedaddled into the long grass. Search as I could I did not find another trace of them. Quite astonishing to have a crowd of chicks at your feet one moment and in a trice—nothing. An achievement innate to all nidifugous broods.

Gladly, the call of the cuckoo is with us again, so often a prompt to the bard:

TO THE CUCKOO
Sweet bird: thy bower is ever green,
Thy sky is ever clear;
Thou hast no sorrow in thy song,
No winter in thy year.

Anonymous

O Blithe new-comer! I have heard,
I hear thee and rejoice.
O cuckoo! Shall I call thee Bird,
Or but a wandering Voice?

William Wordsworth

In my experience, cuckoo sightings have always been erratic from year to year—one summer I might see several, but the next maybe just one or possibly two. This said, in the course of time memorised encounters whether by ear or eye or both, enables one to heighten ones chances of a new meeting in a former locale.

Many years ago, when a lad, I was sitting completely still under a tree-lined hedge facing a wood when to my astonishment a cuckoo flew into a branch almost overhead. It did not make the well-known call but instead uttered a continuous bubbling sound which held me bewitched—it was my first experience of hearing the female cuckoo. Incidentally, shortly after this rendition she flew off, whereupon a shrew, on one of those ceaseless quests for food, trickled over my foot and continued on its way! Such moments are stored for ever . . .

The song thrush, 'with his balanced eloquence of pithy phrase', is dear to my heart; I can recount down through the years and from various locations in the surrounding countryside, when from the top of a tree the tuneful song of an individual has suddenly drawn me to a felicitous peak of emotion.

CHIPPOO-IT! Chippoo-it!
Tio-tew, Tio-tew, Tio-tew! ;
Wee-ploo-ploo! Wee-ploo-ploo! Wee-ploo-ploo!
Tutee-o, Tutee-o!
Tsi-tsi-tew, Tsi-tsi-tew!
Tu-itty, Tu-itty, Tu-itty!
Weet-wee-tew! Weet-wee-tew! Weet-wee-tew! Weet-wee-tew!
Wit-wit-whit-wit-wit!
Pretty! Pretty!

Walter Garstang

How easily I recall the time, many years since, when, sheltering temporarily from a sudden light shower under a hedgetop sycamore, a blackbird had the same objective, arrowing in to perch a few feet above me. Then, it began to sing out its rich ringing notes 'overflowing my already brimming exultancy for these special times'.

Cow parsley is coming to the fore, its white umbels attracting increasing numbers of insects. One of the earliest flowering grasses, the meadow foxtail, shows . . .

The larva of the lunar underwing moth is anomalous: it is on the point of pupating, having fed (incredibly) on meadow grass throughout the winter months, in complete contrast to normal insect behaviour.

In one of two local haunts the pied flycatchers are back. Here in the estate's woodlands, the provision and maintenance of nesting boxes provides a wonderful opportunity to acquaint oneself with an attractive and lovely summer visitor whose presence is thinly scattered throughout the United Kingdom.

51

At month's end, as I look down over the headland, a circling flock of hirundines are below me. For the first time I witness together swallows, house martins and sand martins. They are hawking the gorse-clad slopes, which are alive with insects. When catching the direct sunlight the backs of the swallows fairly gleam.

Two chrysalids kept for months in a jar in my study have hatched, and I marvel at the beautiful shape and colouring of both privet and elephant hawk moths.

The early thorn moth, with closed wings diagonally contoured, can be expected to appear now. There is a second generation on the wing during high summer.

On the inside of the window rest a common yellow ophion, a large ichneumon fly with long antennae. I had seen another of its kind in late autumn of the preceding year at the same window-pane.

Soon to come out of hibernation are the queen wasps, *Vespula vulgaris* and *Vespula germanica*. I have often found these (almost identical) insects together in woodpiles, alongside lacewings and cluster flies. In the same sanctuary spiders prey on the queen wasps, sucking out the body fluids to leave just the shell of the victim. Those queens that have survived will now be actively seeking out nesting quarters where the first 'worker' eggs are deposited—the nuclei for the bustling summertime populations. A populous queendom it will be.

Palpable are the chants and anxieties of the ancients as a cast of darkness obscures the moon. With the lunar eclipse complete, the Halle-Bopp comet's fiery trail (in fact composed of icy dust, stretching for millions of kilometres behind it), as it follows its north-westerly course in the late evening sky, charts time and distance of prodigious measure. And proclaims our vulnerability to cosmic disaster: our Earth, sole planet of organisms wiped out, in galactic standing, as easily and as unmourned as a fly swatted by a human hand. The lording presence of humankind becomes as vulnerable as a meadow of wildflowers. We are irretractably caught up in the 'scheme of things'—indivisible, a microscopic virus could just as easily put paid to our reign.

The vigour of fresh plantlife effectively floods the jubilant eye and spirit as much as it covers the countryside scene.

WITH HEARING ACUTE, EYESIGHT KEEN,
APPRECIATION DEVOUT, I AM THE RICHEST MAN ALIVE

MAY

There is a freshness that one can almost grasp,
a vigour in one's stride and uberous Joy in living.
The dawn chorus—salvoes of Joy at the vortex of life.

s it possible that a month in any other land can match, let alone surpass, our May for its subtle infusion of fullness? And is there any greater mis-judgement than to lose, through slumber, even one note of the early morning salute?

Snow-banks of hawthorn blossom, heavy with scent, like a magnet draw honeybees by the score. Horse chestnut trees are a picture, holding up their pink and white candles.

That sturdy water plant, the yellow flag, flowers in ponds and river margins where mallard and moorhen and, increas-ingly, Canada geese nest. A pair of mute swans have nested regularly in amongst clumps of these concealing plants on a holm in the river; marsh marigolds, also widely known as kingcups are in eye-catching flower along the same habitat.

Further butterfly species are appearing: the orange tip, common and holly blues, and large and small whites. The first mentioned is denoted, in the male only, by orange patch-es on the tips of the forewings. It is a real charmer, perhaps observed during a lower hedgerow dalliance with the small white lookalike female, herself seeking out garlic mustard, cuckoo flower and pennycress on which to secure the grooved skittle-shaped eggs.

The common blue is a typical *thermophile*, more numerous during the forthcoming summer months where its low flight over short distances is part of the close-cropped, grassy-sloped scene. The eggs are deposited on bird's foot trefoil and rest harrow, the food-plants of the slug-like larva. A beautiful little species, quite the study for a recumbent lepidopterist on a sun-filled day. In its quick and erratic flight the holly blue also puts in its first appearance, and is quite likely to visit the flower garden . . .

Most of the large white and small white butterflies have recently hatched from chrysalids that have survived the late autumn and winter, strung to silken pads from under window sills and shed roof eaves. Some forty years ago the village garden fete held a competition for the child who could collect the most 'cabbage-whites'—there were quite a few entrants. In those days these—and other—species thronged the summer hedgerows and meadows and collecting a jamjar full was not considered a Ulyssean task. But herbicides and pesticides have put paid to such abundance . . .

> Among the changing months,
> May stands confest
> The sweetest, and in fairest
> colours dressed.
>
> *James Thomson* (1700–1748)

Thomson's *Seasons* ranked him amongst the world's greatest nature poets, and rightly so. His succinct observations encapsulate what we all admire about sweetest, fairest May:

> This glorious rush of life.

Amongst plants, birds and insects alike are to be found exhibited the richest and freshest of colours. Red campion, common vetch, hedgerow cranesbill and herb robert are the bright new (evanescent) flowers of our hedgerows.

And whether it be chaffinch or eider duck, bullfinch or jay, during the breeding season the males of the bird world cannot fail to catch the eye as they sport their finest plumage in the driving quest for a mate.

I hold that a meadowful of buttercups fully deserves eulogy: I have many and oft set eyes on fields awash with their rich golden yellow. And peeking through the tall stems from the grass understorey are the crimson clovers that I am much attracted by. Abundant on the lower slopes of one such field with its butter-hued harvest are early purple orchids. Drifting over this living picture from its song-post the sun-steeped lilting phrases of a brilliant yellow hammer serve to both complement and excite my feelings.

Thrift leads a trail of pink along the cliff walks. Red campion shows in any number of locations, vigorous in some areas, less so elsewhere: as with other plants, their height and strength is determined by the aspect (sun or shade, exposed or sheltered) and the condition of the soil. The rich colour of both plant species is soon faded by the streaming sunlight that conversely darkens the leaves of the trees. There is a matchless almond scent from the golden-yellow nectareous gorse.

1st May. Glorious weather. Travelling along a country road in a sheltered valley. A lush stretch of hedgerow is holding the attention of an inordinate number of orange tip butterflies—full of garlic mustard. Beautiful. Further on I happen upon my first ever patch of Solomon's Seal, growing on the unused margin of land between road and hedge. A stoat, doubtless with young to feed, crosses the road in front of me with a mouse firmly held in its jaws.

Every minute spent out-of-doors is vindicated. Before me lies both the expected and the unexpected—a reunion with many species and a never ending introduction to others.

A giddy profusion of insects; a slow-worm in the hedge; the rich notes of a blackcap; a solitary starling vents its feelings with an adroit use of tongue and nasal play that I have never encountered before; on a telephone wire directly overhead to where I am sitting a male swallow—longer forked tail than female—twitters at great speed, the frequent snapping of the bill integral to the melody; on separate occasions house sparrows are seen in the ditch tugging at reedmace—for nest lining material—and likewise in my garden tugging at the dead twigs of a climber for use as the framework for another nest.

Great black-backed gulls have flown far inland and are feasting on the carcass of a lamb.

8p.m.   A lizard is espied on a south-facing hedge, catching the last warming rays of the sinking sun. Moths are appearing in steadily increasing numbers. Speckled yellow moths can be seen during the day along woodland edges and hedgerows. The common or garden swift is attracted to light. The ruby-tail, order *Hymenoptera,* family *Chrysididae* is a 'jewel'—emerald head and thorax and ruby abdomen glint in the sun as it rests for a short while on the stone wall. Its rich beauty belies its habits: it preys on other species of *Hymenoptera.*

The ground under a hawthorn tree is sprinkled with pink seeds.

Now the spindlewood flowers. Red valerian (which is sometimes white) has become a floral feature on the tops and sides of walls and along the wayside. Much visited by bees, butterflies and other insects, it was brought here round about the fifteenth century from central and southern Europe. It makes a welcome ornament.

The rowan blossoms locally, but this is close to sea level. The rowans—and hawthorns—of the high moor will take a little longer to appear in all their glory. A month when herbage and grasses grow thick and tall. 'Laid-up' fields of grass reflecting the sun and bending uniformly with the breezes become scintillating seas. Many hedgerows are afroth with cow parsley or ribboned with red campion.

Every parish beckons a lifetime's absorption in the study of its wildflowers.

> It is, I find, in zoology as it is in botany; all nature is so full that that district produces the greatest variety which is the most examined.

> *Gilbert White (Letter XX)*

Deep in the forestry plantation a solitary tall ash is haloed with sunlight. Nearby a roe buck is disturbed and, gazelle-like, leaps across the path and crashes away into the bowels of the wood. Yellow pimpernel and herb bennet are seen herein and along the woodland edge flutter green-veined whites. In full view of a blue sky and beating sun the lush herbage and grasses, both on hedgebank and along the footpath, in warm cheek-caressing wafts, infuse the air with aromatic freshness.

The pageantry of life—fragile complex and absorbing life: for all that is seen and noticed the greater part passes unrecorded, each day an unwritten volume. And in describing the sights and sounds of glorious Maytime we struggle to do it justice. Only birdsong can articulate the wondrous pleasures of creativity.

And splendour, splendour everywhere.

In the night sky, hanging prominently in the north west, is a twinkling jewel. Venus, brilliant Venus—26 million miles away at its closest position to Earth—cannot fail to engage the eye. At May's opening this 'wandering star' sets after midnight, but before its close it will be appearing even before sun-down as the lantern of early evening . . .

. . . a lantern to the stars deep above in the celestial heavens; in galaxies; trillions of galaxies contracting or expanding in the mind-floundering immensity of space. And to think, if we travelled at the speed of light—186,273 miles per second—to cross our own galaxy would entail a voyage lasting ten thousand years.

Our beautiful Earth, where 99% of life forms had perished before homo sapiens came of age, is but a grain of sand in the ocean of space and time. The mind is crushed by the magnitude of creativity; any thoughts of superiority we may harbour are pulverized by the realisation of our insignificance. . .

Apart from Man, no being wonders at its own existence.

Arthur Schopenhauer

2nd May. After distinguishing the sandpiper by its typical dipping action, I started up the estuary and was delighted by the overhead flypast of my first swifts of the year. Three pairs of scimitar wings return to cleave the Devonshire ether—another gratifying reunion. My diary shows the swifts are forty days behind the sand martins and twenty-five days later than the first swallow. Reaching the reserve with its mud channels and salting guts, I adjust the binoculars in order to confirm the identification of the group of waders that have veered away to the inner lagoon. I count some 60 whimbrel. The smaller size, shorter decurved bill and noticeable head-stripes are telling differences from cousin curlew. Watching these birds of passage feed I conclude that they are more animated than curlews ever are: not without verve are they probing and advancing along the shelving mud, at the waterline and in the shallows of the lagoon.

The whimbrel, having flown from the wintering quarters along the west coast of Africa, were now refuelling for the onward journey to the breeding grounds of Scandinavia. Is this the selfsame flock I will encounter on the return journey, logged 14th August? The birds do not linger long. Taking advantage of the weather conditions, they will determinedly continue the final leg of their journey—even through the night, I am almost certain.

A week later and strong winds and heavy rain—in twelve hour valediction—pummel the tender new foliage. Bud cases, leafage and blossom sprinkle down, littering the ground under the trees. More in keeping with an autumnal scene the finches gather for the pickings. But the whimbrel are at least long gone, escaped to cooler but calmer climes. . .

16th May. On the common I note the splendour of hawthorn blossom. Sycamore also. Bluebells, the first foxgloves, lousewort, cow parsley, pignut. Pearl-bordered fritillaries (there is a string of seven 'pearls' on the underside of the hind wings) patrol a section of sunlit footpath, seeing off any insect trespasser. A freshly emerged speckled yellow moth has met an early fate and is now being hauled along an ant trail. Damselflies: banded, red and *Coenagrion puella*. 'Dancing' low over the crab apple branches are *Adela viridella*, family *Incurvariidae*, metallic hued 'bright moths', the males of which have exceptionally long antennae.

On the steep-sloped side of the common at the end of May the Manna Ash (Flowering ash) is a-cloud with flower.

> The fisher of the solitudes
> Stands by the river's brim.

Mary Howitt

59

Standing on the sill of the weir the heron and carrion crow are enacting a scene akin to the salmon-catching bears of North America. Brown trout fry, just a few inches in length, are attempting to leap the weir and the grey heron catches several by anticipating their movements or picking up those that have got stranded on the muddied dry rocks at the edge of the spillover. Yet another is caught in mid-air as it makes a prodigious yet fateful leap.

All the while the carrion crow—though the first to anticipate a meal here—is merely a spectator to the skills of the specialist fisher.

It seems there are small clusters of yellow eggs, similar to those of ladybirds, attached to the underside of almost every dock plant. And just as numerous above, on the upper leaves, are the glinting leaf beetles, with metallic green and copper-coloured elytra, which laid them. (The elytra are the modified forewings—of beetles—used to shield the 'flight-wings'.) The egg-bearing females now have bloated abdomens which tell them apart from the males that can be observed already coupling, or in search of the unattached. What is their given name?

After much frantic searching of reference works I discovered that the dock leaf beetle is simply named as such: family *Chrysomelidae*, genus *Chrysomela*. Finding an insect, or plant or whatever, that you cannot name even after initial research from one's small library of reference works can be the most frustrating of times. But once, through resolve, the species is traced, then there is a deal of satisfaction that is most lifting.

With the countryside a suffusion of plant-growth the insect world stirs into action; thick with numbers, particularly along the lush sea-scape of grass fields, moving wave-like in the breeze, laid-up for silage or haymaking, is that notable diptera, the St Mark's fly, *Bibio marci*, so called because of its appearance close to 25th April (St Mark's day). Being a large, black insect with characteristic 'hanging-flight', with legs held a-dangle, it is easily recognized.

The males swarm at first over the lethargic females sitting in the grass; eventually, aerial mating takes place. It is a member of the family *Bibionidae*, of which there are eighteen species, and is seen for only a matter of weeks, though the progeny will provide the same display during the same weeks in the following year. One of the sepsid flies (from the family *Sepsidae*, noted for their ant-like bodies) swarms over similar haunts as the former. Both are almost certain sights for this month's rambler.

The larva of the hover fly *Syrphus balteatus* (family *Syrphidae*, with some five thousand different species) feeds on aphids. In its final stage it becomes an altogether fascinating subject in gardens and elsewhere, the blurring wing-beat enabling it to manoeuvre at will, one moment statically examining a flower head and the next jigging around like a miniature UFO on a reconnaissance mission.

Seven-spot ladybird beetles have been in low-key activity since March but their numbers will soon multiply several times over once the developing larvae, feeding voraciously on the aphids and greenfly that can infest rose bushes, have pupated and changed into adults.

In the oak trees, of which there are several types, 'oak apples' are appearing. This growth has been promoted by the gall wasp *Biorrhiza pallida*. Other gall wasps that attack the oak are marble gall, *(Andricus kollarii)*, spangle gall, *(Neuroterus quercushbaccarumli)*, and the silk button gall *(Neuroterus nimismalis)*. Gall wasps are tiny bodied insects of the family *Cynipidae*, and to absorb the complexity of their life-cycles is a truly head-spinning exercise.

It is best left for me to say that it would be most enlightening for the inquisitive mind to read-up on the subject of asexual (parthenogenetic) insect broods: to glean knowledge of certain species that can dictate the sex of a whole generation. Gripping!

When I was a child it was still customary to take sprigs of oak to school to commemorate King Charles II's escape from the enemy, and very often these held the soft-white, freshly formed 'oak-apples', although at the time I was oblivious to the insect's handiwork.

OAK APPLE DAY

Charles the Second was born on May 29th, 1630. It was on the day after the Battle of Worcester, which took place on September 3rd, 1651, that Charles, in the company of Colonel Careless, climbed into a large oak tree. But if he had actually done so at the date on which this was to be later commemorated—his birth-date—the oak's foliage would not have been sufficiently advanced to afford much concealment. A now forgotten jingle repeated by schoolboys of old went:

> Twenty-ninth of May,
> Oak Apple Day.
> If you don't give us a holiday,
> We'll all run away.

Two further wasp's galls are found on dog rose and these, to give them their popular names, are the easily detected robin's pincushion—so named for obvious reasons—and the spiked pea, which is found on the leaves.

At last, after its 'pressed' rosette leaves have featured for so many weeks along the coastal path, the buckshorn plantain finally pushes up its flower spikes. Here it is companion to numerous other flowering plants . . .

Thrift, sea campion, ground ivy, sheep's sorrel, horseshoe vetch, biting stonecrop, spring cinquefoil and burnet rose all have a hold, or at least a niche, on the coastal margins.

Burnet rose shares a space on the cliff-top slope with western gorse, a similarly low bush (serotinous in botanical parlance) that flowers very late in the season and on into autumn. Appearing contentious, even so, a number of the *Rosa pimpinellifolia* have threaded their thickly bristled stems through the branches of the abutting gorse and, in an overlay of decorous cream and pink flowers, attract the attention of bees and tiny insects.

To the leavening sun the bracken unfurls its fronds; black bryony, with leaves agloss, twines upwards to the hedgetop and the 'popping' contraction of gorse pods broadcasts dark seeds.

Most trees are now full-leafed. The palpate leaves on the

sycamores often incline to form 'wigwams'; the elliptical leaves of the broadleafed lime are often translucent. On a circular walk taken regularly throughout the year I pass a fine red oak tree planted at the driveway entrance to a country estate. The deeply lobed leaves of this introduced species are much larger than our common oak. When first out the leaves are orange but soon change to 'oak' green. It is well in advance of *Quercus robur,* whose leaves are only just beginning to open.

The pale yellowish-green clusters of fruit discs on the wych elm are slowly being immersed in the foliage. Bay laurel has blossomed and soon the fig-like fruits will appear. As beaked hawksbeard seeds along its wayside haunts, lesser hawkbit comes into flower. And linnets feast off the dandelion 'clocks'.

All too soon wildflowers in their ephemerality arise, flower, seed and wither away. To minimize the chance of competition from similar species in the attraction of insects, each plant times its appearance to side-step another. Whether or not this organised 'randomness' is indeed their secret of survival, through a smooth continuity, weeks on end, the spent plants concur to a voidless passing.

I have no illusions about my botanising expertise and to me the white umbellifers are a particular minefield of similarity. However, the rough chervil's liking for shade lends itself to swift identification—after I have made notes on its structure and habitat and, on returning home, consulting my field guide. Students of heredity could do worse than check out the *Umbelliferae.*

Insects—particularly the *Diptera* or true-flies—are out perforce. On a footpath through the meadow grass moths are noticed, and Timothy grass and the less obvious field woodrush on which the ants will gather and take the seeds. A small copper is seen, then another and an orange tip also. Along the hawthorned lane the red-tailed bumble bees have recently appeared, much later risers, it seems, than *Bombus terrestris*—the yellow-banded.

The hoary and ribwort plantain line the wayside: displaying their 'choir-boy ruffs' on the flower spikes, which in the former are longer than the latter (though both are much shorter than those of the greater plantain, which appears a little later). Bugle is also now at its most prolific and best.

Everywhere, balls of spiderlings hatching.

Tunnels of green formed by the beeches.

I find white common comfrey, white valerian and white campion.

The common names for many of our 2,500 moth species deserve a special mention, for these are very descriptive, picturesque labels indeed: e.g. Chinese character, coxcomb prominent, footman, lutestring, vapourer, tussock, umber, engrailed, wainscot, merveille du jour. The Victorian entomologists and collectors, from whom the great bulk of the names derive, have indeed left a wonderful legacy. And what do we have now at the lighted window. A Hebrew Character. And among the numbers of moths now logged are the aforementioned coxcomb prominent with brindled beauty, muslin, angle shades and buff tip. And of course many smaller day-flying pugs, waves and carpets: and micro-moths a-plenty.

Prior to entering the wood I check an old and rotting oak branch lying in a sunspot on the hedgetop. But no grass snake today, though I have observed it here, partially coiled, in the three previous years. A stride further and on a nettle an insect with long antennae. It is a moth, *Nemophera degeerella*—from the family *Incurvariidae*—all of which possess long antennae. This fellow, the most interesting, has the longest, an incredible three times its body length.

A leat that diverts water from the woodland-bordering stream is cloaked with flowering common water-crowfoot. Entering this cover I espy the unmistakable woodruff, its whorls of leaf clusters up the stem reminding me (rather obliquely I suppose) of yellow-wort. Apparently, in days gone by woodruff was collected and dried, thereafter put in amongst linen for its hayfield scent. Here also is sanicle—hardly representative of its *Umbelliferae* grouping flowering within a few feet of the woodruff. Outside, on the open meadow slope, the primroses have a surprise in their midst. One of their kind, with pretensions of being an oxlip or cowslip, holds ten flower-heads from a solitary ten-inch (20 cm) stalk.

In the plantation ride pearl-bordered fritillaries are feeding on the flowering bugle. On the upside, oddly, of a bramble leaf a moth, later identified as *Tortricodes alternella,* is seen at rest. It had been disturbed from a more concealed daytime retirement, had it not? On the branch tips of the pines I admire the fresh green and tactility of the new needles . . .

In a ponded bend of the small stream a movement caught the eye, a tadpole or two. Towards one of them, like a dragging anchor on the seabed, advanced a tiny knot of debris, in fact *Linnephilus lunatus,* the larva of a caddis fly . . .

Goosegrass, that sticky-burred, tentacled plant, is opening its white flowers along the hedgerows. On more open ground the ribwort plantain stands erect.

Gorse and broom cloak the slopes with glorious yellow and the delicious almond scent attracts bees and insects—and Reynard who, lying in the grassy space fronting the sun, appears as appreciative as anyone. Broom is often found in woodland clearings where it is a bonus to the wandering bees and insect-feeding smaller birds. The hardy gorse can bloom at any time during the year, though it is never quite so prolific as now. "Kissing's out of season when gorse is out of bloom!" they say.

Furze is the regional label for gorse and there is a locality nearby so named; undoubtedly a connection arises as there is a fair amount of scrubland here. Gorse, or furze (the shorter, western gorse is found on the moor) can thrive in the very shallowest of soil, surviving, nay flourishing, even where mechanical diggers on road widening schemes have left just a dry shale surface.

The drooping flower clusters of the sycamore make it a veritable 'promised land' for myriads of bees and insects and the ideal place for the amateur entomologist.

A browning of blossom.

Appearing in substantial numbers for certain weeks along the broader streams and rivers are the 'gauzy' long tailed mayflies. There are many species but most have hatched out of pupae from nymphs that have lived underwater for some time, having fed on detritus. Mayflies are unique in the insect world in that, once having emerged from a pupa into the perfect insect or imagine, go through another rapid moult—the dun or sub-imagine becoming a shiny-imagine or spinner—to live out an ephemeral life-span. This short span is frequently pared even shorter by the acrobatic trout, the familiar concentric splashes betraying the presence of these agile fish.

The aiderfly, a less delicate species, is also abundant on the same waters, and likes to rest on the bankside foliage.

Some deciduous woods are carpeted in deep blue, so thickly grow the single-stemmed bluebells, filling the air with their heavy hyacinth perfume. In those same woods can also be found the delicate white anemone, or wildflower, growing in abundance in shady places . . . all-pervasive.

The sloping meadow imbibes the midday sun. Presently, a distinct whining from nearby flowerheads swivels the eye to the hovering common bee-fly, unique with its spindly legs and long proboscis, attached to a small furry body—it is a picture of innocence. Not so. The female drops her eggs near the nests of mining bees and the hatched larvae enter and destroy the tenants. The 'common' bee-fly seems to me very local and not widely distributed in the area; at least, my sightings are few and far between.

A regular sight in the garden though are the red velvet mites *Eutrombidium rostratus*, of the class *Arachnidae*, sometimes seen in groups milling around—especially on stones and paths. These are predatory creatures, clinging to the bodies of their prey. The snipe fly can also be seen in the garden, where it will alight, always face down, on a tree or fence—an attractive, elongated and slender fly. The harvestman *Leiabunum rotundum* is also quite a common feature of gardens and, being mainly nocturnal and drawn to light, often 'bounces' into hallways and kitchens. It is another arachnid—looking like a cross between spider and crane-fly—but, like the velvet mite, not in the same group as the spiders, and feeds on both dead and living insects.

Noted on a number of plant stalks along country lanes and the like are masses of froth. 'Cuckoo spit' contains a green nymph, which in its protective environment sucks out and feeds on the sap of the plant. In time this creature emerges as the common froghopper *Philaenus spumarius;* hard to detect until one brushes against foliage whereupon it catapults away . . .

Sand martins are now nesting. A colony in my district have patronized a certain length of riverbank for several decades, regardless of the winter floodwater's continual erosion of the bank. And of the past attentions of egg-collecting youths, happily no longer practised.

So here, the sand martins fortuitously hold their own. A hundred yards or so further up-river from the sand martin colony a pair of dippers are raising a brood from a nest built on the outer ledge, under the railway bridge. Strange to ponder that the dipper, noted for its usually retiring countenance, should choose such a noise-pummelling site; the chicks in particular have to brave the thunderous sound of locomotive and carriages directly overhead. Apocolyptically noisy. (From practically the moment they stand the chicks are given to rhythmic genuflection, the mark of the species.) The nearest some people ever get to viewing the dipper is a streak of white—displayed by the throat and breast—as the surprised bird flies off at speed.

Unlike the martins, swallows are not communal, and the solitary nest is positioned on a beam in a barn, shippen or other easily entered outhouse. I once had the amusing experience of watching a pair of swallows squabbling over the primary feather of a farmyard hen. Later, on inspecting the nest of one of the combatants, the hindering, over-large feather overlapping the sides suggested it had been but a false trophy.

Swallows and the two species of martin have elongated eggs, and whilst the former are white with brown spots those of the latter are pure white. It is a general rule that eggs laid in dark environments remain uncoloured, camouflage being irrelevant. This is the case with the tunnel-nesting kingfisher and treehole-nesting woodpeckers and titmice. Therefore, it is intriguing to find that the wood pigeon lays WHITE eggs—on a shallow, twig-latticed platform—quite detectable to the upward eye. Yet it manages to survive exceedingly well.

There is a 'battle royale' as nuthatch and green woodpecker spin earthwards but, in this case, the ambitious 'squatter' does not manage to relieve the latter of its arduously chiselled freehold.

You have seen the swift beating its scimitar wings, rapidly climbing up the sky. Then, a streamlined monoplane, in one great downward curve, slicing through the air. And that exhilarating 'screel' as it sweeps through the nesting area, as though to cry, 'Look at me, I'm the fastest thing on wings'. These meteors nest in crevices under the roofs of old buildings to which they return annually. The nursery is nothing more than a rather makeshift pile of straw or hay, mixed with feathers which are caught in flight. The house sparrow and starling utilise similar sites and are equally shoddy builders.

The wren is an adroit nest-builder, placing the dome-shaped construction of grass, moss and leaves, lined with wool and feathers, in a hole in a stone wall or bank. One precariously sited nest of *Troglodytes troglodytes* was found on the swifter flowing side of a stream, secured between the turf overhang and the top edge of the bank. The wren often betrays its nest by 'churring' at passers-by, when to remain silent would not have drawn attention to the source of its anxiety. A charming little bird and another firm favourite, our craky.

The last twenty years have shown a marked increase in the buzzard population. The 'Englishman's eagle' had been affected by a scarcity of rabbits through the nation-wide spread of myxomatosis, but also by the misguided attentions of game-keepers and farmers who shot and poisoned the noble bird. I am pleased to say that there are now several nesting pairs in my district, indeed the whole of the county is well populated. The honey buzzard breeds occasionally in south Devon, where I have seen it in flight over the forest. When lemmings are scarce in its homeland the rough-legged buzzard just might put in an appearance here in North Devon during wintertime . . .

On one unforgettable occasion I found a buzzard's bulky nest in an oak tree and decided, for once, to climb up to it for close examination of the contents. About half way up the tree

I encountered the nest hole of wild honey bees. But after a momentary hesitation, and swallowing hard, I carefully negotiated this hazard and reached my destination without further ado. The nest contained four large, off-white eggs tinted with green, two of which were more heavily blotched with brown. To my astonishment I saw that the exterior of the nest was carefully screened with freshly plucked stems of ivy. Clearly the majestic birds were thorough in their home-making. Hearing the swoosh of wings I looked across into the adjoining tree and found a pair of sharp yellow eyes glaring back at me. My approach had ushered the sitting bird from the warm clutch, now she was back, watching and waiting. Not to delay the incubation further I at once descended the tree and moved quickly away.

On another occasion in a broad-leaved wood—in July—the trees above me were suddenly filled with buzzards, some making their entry into the wide open world. There were five immature ones in all, and their plaintive cries—one of summer's hallmarks hereabouts—were answered by the parents, wheeling high above the tree-tops. When a pair of buzzards are in the air together they take reverse courses, crossing and recrossing each others' spirals with a balletic grace.

The nest of the magpie is hardly ever examined for it is a fortress against all likely enemies, being built in impenetrable thorn trees and most sturdily secured with sticks and at its base roots and mud. Dome-shaped, the entrance hole is halfway up one side.

In a small woodland valley barely out of sight of the estuary (where I have encountered and recorded a great variety of plants, birds and animals), two pairs of shelduck are nesting. The rabbit-warrened floor of the wood has served the breeding ducks well over the years but I have yet to witness the wonderful spectacle of the courtship display therein. Whenever the shelduck return to their nest sites in the wood several circuits are flown to confirm that there are no prying eyes and it is safe to land.

Swifts—

skating in majestic arcs upon the blue plane of the sky

(from 'Hard Facts' – *Howard Spring*)

—soundlessly trawl the upper air. My gaze reaches six miles beyond—to the cirrocumulus ice-clouds that form thin patterned sheets, superimposed on the liquid azure. Billowing clouds, 'moving mountains', appear, then presently clear to sheets of cracked ice, clearing again to form mackerel, framed with the clear azure and on . . . The play of the sun and colour on cloudscape always thrills the upturned eye . . .

With an in-coming call note to its brooding mate the male green woodpecker settles as if with magnetic clamping on to the branch a little below the nest hole. It is in vivid peak condition—the deep crimson crest seems to be of a sealing wax consistency. He darts up and, with zygodactyl toes, fastens to the tree trunk—half a metre above the nest hole. Seconds later the anticipating female peers out of the hole, emerges and quietly slips away. Instantly he backs down the trunk in fluent hops and disappears into the entrance hole for a stint of egg sitting . . .

Where once the coal-fired power station stood, nature has reclaimed the derelict site for her own. Always the opportunists, gorse and sallow have swiftly colonised the adjacent ash-beds, but there is room aplenty for an interesting array of wildflowers—especially marsh orchids—also, in turn drawing a multitude of insects. A cuckoo has more or less taken up its annual summer residence here. I come to within sixty paces of him as, with wings held typically a-droop, he 'implores' from the top of the gorse bush—spell-binding.

A gathering of small tortoiseshell butterflies disports over the nettle patch. From their midst a pair suddenly spiral skywards at a rush: ardour-driven procreation that will soon become manifest with colonies of grey caterpillars on the leaves of the nettles below.

May comes sweet and complete in every detail. Along every lane and hedgerow bank spring a thousand small and seldom considered things—Nature's embroidery, to finish off her festal robe to perfection . . .

from 'A Country Calendar'– *Flora Thompson*

If one bottled the essence of May the ingredients would surely be sap-fresh grasses—and rushes—hawthorn blossom and cow parsley.

Panicles of grasses acknowledge the resurgent air.

And a man, you know, has just so many May
mornings in his life. So few, rather.

from 'The Road of a Naturalist' – *Donald Culross Peattie*

From an overhanging branch high above the country road a caterpillar of green oak tortrix moth dangles from a long length of silken thread. Why—to escape a predator?

Further on, a sight which thank goodness I now rarely encounter, a rabbit with myxomatosis (carried from diseased to healthy rabbit by the rabbit flea) immobile and grotesque in its suffering. Such a sight always takes me back to my childhood and my recoiling from a roadside victim of this horrible Brazilian disease, 'mixee' . . .

Introduced by the Normans some 700 years ago, the rabbit population became a valuable resource both for the landowner and, more importantly, the land workers and country folk generally. However the brutal steel gin traps and wires used to procure this free meal ensnared great numbers of the rabbit's natural predators such as stoats, weasels and foxes.

My father tells me that in his young days, when he himself laid several gin-traps, he would ask of his peers on their catch and often the reply would be something like "half a dozen rabbits and twenty legs"—the legs of animals other than rabbits which had excruciatingly gnawed their way to a short-lived freedom. With an imbalance becoming inevitable the rabbit population exploded, and became a serious pest to agriculture. In the early 1950s myxomatosis was introduced to curb the population and has remained, to this day, the scourge of this endearing rodent. The dark side of nature!

At some point in the distant future the earth might again become flowerless: the beauty of wildflowers just might be sacrificed to nature's ever dynamic processes. And the composite dandelion tribe are leading the way. This month flowering at their most plentiful—a golden wash of colour—

dandelions *Taraxacum* Section *Vulgaria* have been accorded the status has one of the 'high' plants; high interpreted as having evolved its life mechanisms relatively late, with the corollary that its survival seems all the more assured. Its ubiquity is owed, in no short measure, to lack of sexuality—the dandelion is sexless!

> It is as if the dandelion has said to itself, I am perfect: as I am no more mixing heredities, no need now of insect-assisted cross-fertilization.

from *Devolution* in 'The Great Chain of Life' – *Joseph Wood Krutch*

The 'flower-head' no longer serves any utilitarian purpose. Nature permits no waste for any length of time; flowers might be abandoned altogether in the far off future. Most sinister.

In one of a number of the estate woodlands to the north-east of a historic house—run by the National Trust—an avenue of full grown sycamores over 100 ft tall are in marked contrast to those seen growing on the hedge earlier that day. Some books deride the sycamore for its detrimental effect on other plantlife, but I cannot do other than sing the praises of whoever planted these magnificent 'cathedrals' fifty or sixty years since. These selfsame trees seem to whisper to me 'look at what we become when given the opportunity'. A moral there somewhere.

If the sky falls we catch larks

SUMMER

The synthesizing sun balms the soul.

 ith nature at the zenith of intense richness and diversity the delicate freshness of former months has burgeoned full-bodied. Plant life rears to the alchemy of sunshine, rainfall and soil.

I observe the countryside in summer raiment with eyes that can never hope to capture the full abundance and melodrama of life, yet which exult in all they see—*multum in parvo.*

> We think the ancients were foolish who worshipped the sun. I would worship it for ever if I had grace to do so.
>
> *Henry Thoreau*

> For inspiration, for beauty, for health and refreshment, for a sense of freedom and the enlargement of the soul, is there anything like the summer sky? How it attracts us! Draws us out of doors! How it rewards us!
>
> *John Pulsford*

Though

> Human thoughts and imaginings written down are pale and feeble in bright summer light.
>
> 'Meadow Thoughts' – *Richard Jefferies*

The unrivalled, but sadly now rare, scent of new-made hay and the perfumes of numerous wild flowers permeate the sultry air. Through the shimmering midday heat the droop-headed corn turns a ripened yellow. The call of the warbler is distinct, yet softly ringing, from the majestic oak orb'd by a sky wisped with cloud, where swallow, martin and swift weave ethereal tapestries.

With wings of untouchable delicate beauty butterflies caress the aerial radiance with the robust hawker dragonflies unbending to the lilt of gentle breezes. The lacewing's venated tracery is steeped in light. By slow-flowing, sparkling water courses iridescent damselflies disport above iris, rush and associated herbage.

Where the bee sucks . . .

Interwoven or sentinel, wildflowers wreathe the countryside and frustrate the observer with a poor head for names. The various parsleys, meadowsweet, honeysuckle, woundwort, helloborine, orchid, vetchling, hawkweeds, rest harrow, clovers, trefoil, mouse-ear, hedge bedstraw, valerian, scabious, betony, knapweed and flowering bramble are but a few of the hundreds of plant species seducing insects into unwitting pollination.

The foxgloves are jostled at intervals by the heavyweight bumblebees, collecting pollen and nectar and returning to the underground chamber where the nest of grass and moss conceals the young in their waxen cells.

Sweet tunes from the constantly rising and 'parachuting' meadow pipits. An embodied joy, the skylark—heaven's minstrel, the sun's emissary, flamelet of song, pilgrim of the sky, feathered lyric—the metaphors abound, rises into the blueness to perform a cataract of song. A voice which transcends the social spectrum, noted and beloved by all through its rain of melody . . .

The cooing of wood-pigeon or the humming from innumerable insect wing-beats with distant-echoing cuckoo calls instil a sweet suspension. The mercurial trout rises from its pebble-lined riverbed as the spotted flycatcher, from the aspen at the rim of the bank, makes an outward looping sally and 'snaps' a fly.

The summertime countryside fairly teems with life, appeased only by an elastic daytime and a dusk-night ever astir with foraging inhabitants of the dark: and moths, those beauties largely unviewed, save when attracted to illumination.

> If we should have a genuine torment let us wish for too much time.
>
> *Goethe*

But the clenched-fist of nature—forever in the wings of the theatre of life—is easily summoned. A louring sky portends the booming storm which arrests a landscape that becomes violated by a power strike that cleaves the great tree.

Meteorites—space debris, perhaps from the birth of the solar system—hurtle through the vastness of space and time. But earth's gravitational pull intercepts the incalculable journey and, retrieved from the grass, the silver-shot ore is held in the palm of the hand.

The twinkling heavens and our place in the welter of cosmic illusion imbues the human mind. And a late bird

> wings across the bright moon . . .

SUNRISE TO SUNSET, SUNSET TO SUNRISE,
NATURE IS ALL A-BUSTLE.

JUNE

And what is so rare as a day in June?
Then, if ever, come perfect days;
Then Heaven tries earth if it be in tune,
And over it softly her warm ear lays.
'Vision of Sir Launfal' *Lowell*

ndeed. Shorn flocks of excitable ewes with lambs. The sweet scent of elder blossom. Purple 'earth-lodged clouds' of grasses. Ah, subliminal June. On the Burrows I sink into a bed of wildflowers and grasses. A subtle essence, an emanation of wild-pure life, overlays my senses—my eyelids close and

Life's burdens fall, its discords cease,
I lapse into the glad release
Of Nature's own exceeding peace.

Whittier

And yet my hungry curiosity quickly resurfaces:

for the mind is filled with the exceeding beauty of the things, and their great wondrousness and marvel.

Richard Jefferies

Thyme and viper's bugloss, marsh orchid, marsh helleborine, common centuary, eyebright, yellow wort, yellow rattle, ribbed melilot, kidney vetch, self-heal, quaking grass. And grizzled skippers and common blues. And beetles completely red—is it *Coccidula rufa* of the family *Coccinellidae*, incorpo-

76

rating ladybirds? From the sallow carr the calls of warblers. The murmurous air infused with an invisible exploded colossus of insects. Skylarks in the blueness above.

And on and on . . . days that are with me yet.

> The delicacy and beauty of thought or feeling is so extreme that it cannot be inked in . . .

Richard Jefferies

On another day and farther along the coastline, in a small area at the valley bottom, I note green hairstreak and small heath butterflies, spring squill, kidney vetch, sheepsbit scabious, wood sage, yarrow, moorland-evoking bell heather, the silvery-pink thrift, bladder campion.

And new soft shoots on the thicket-forming gorse bushes, intermingling with bramble and blackthorn on the steeply rising sun-drenched slopes, where whitethroats, blackcaps and wrens 'dip and dally': the yellow shell of a brown-lipped grove snail on the hedgebank, a clearwing moth and a silver Y moth. (The latter being one of those barely credible immigrants to these fair shores).

Before the end of May in 1996 I observed a 'fall' of painted lady butterflies near one coastal resort and a week or so into June of that same year it was reported by a villager in mid-Devon, a fellow of the Royal Entomological Society of London no less, that he had witnessed an unbroken flypast of countless thousands of these, from mid-afternoon to dusk—and smaller numbers into the following day.

Although migrations from the continent do take place annually, on a barely perceptible scale, mass movements are few and far between, 1879 and 1903 being of particular note. How I wish I had been privy to such an awe-inspiring spectacle.

During late morning on a section of the high moor, the common heath moths are active in unprecedented numbers about the shrubby plants. Lousewort and milkwort are widespread. A small boggy area near the base of a steep rise harbours the lovely violet-coloured common butterwort. Bog asphodel will soon be in flower 'on the Chains'. Flitting along the tree-lined banks of the coruscating moorland stream a green-veined white butterfly, discordal cell discernible. Bloody-nosed beetle, oak eggar caterpillar, drinker moth also hereabouts.

Cleavers or goosegrass in flower, as is snowberry and olearia or daisy bush. Laurel forming berries. Fruits forming on hawthorn. Sloes green. Satiny oak leaves. Dark leaves on the ash, keys well developed. Each day is filled with fresh delight.

For a few weeks, hairy tare, mingling here and there with meadow vetchling, is the prominent vetch/pea along the flanks of the popular trail—previously a coastal stretch of rail-track. Here we have a haven for the amateur botanist, with a wide variety of wildflowers 'standing to be recognized'.

The occasional yellow flowered spikes of agrimony are admired, the Perforate St John's Wort—with two raised lines down the stem—increasingly common. Mugwort—silvery underside showing when glanced by a passing breeze. Wild carrot is one of the more readily identified *Umbelliferae*, its coarse-hair stems and umbels of uneven petals diagnostic. At sea-level the plants are shorter, stouter and hairier than those of its kind growing at a higher altitude inland. When setting seed the umbels become concave, giving another clear pointer to recognition . . .

. . . the dandelion-like goatsbeard here also, its large clocks (pappose) developing and presenting an obvious on-the-spot explanation for the common name of *Tragopogon pratensis*. Present here also a 'stand' of hedge mustard, tall, stiff, tree-like, with cousin charlock not far away. Some way off but supporting the predominance of the colour yellow is the tall evening primrose. Dwarf mallow and 'fireweed' tend to restore some balance in the colour scheme. The colourful canvas of wildflowers is tempered by the broad brush-strokes of white of the ox-eye daisies, growing in patches and files highlighting the trail.

Yarrow, yellow toadflax, black medick, field bindweed, wall barley and, though partially obscured by grasses, the parasitic common broomrape are all there. The tall square-stemmed figwort appears in small groups along the trail: in such a group three of the plants immediately stand out because they wear the large, conspicuous white with black-and-yellow-dotted caterpillars of the mullein moth. David J. Carter states, in *The Observer's Book of Caterpillars,* that on pupation this species will sometimes remain as long as five years underground before hatching into a perfect insect.

On an umbel of thirty white flowers—one of a group of hemlock water dropwort along the trail, I count seven shield bugs, *Verlusca rhombea,* their diamonded backs glistening.

On the selfsame day the silken webs, and the lackey moth caterpillars that have spun them, are found on blackthorn, hawthorn, oak and sallow.

Walking the footpath at the estuary and scanning the saltmarsh there are contrasting flora, tough and often fleshily structured to withstand this specialized environment—glasswort a prime example. Amidst the 'meadow-like' annual seablite on the saltmarsh rest numbers of partially hidden curlew. Here there are greater sea spurrey, sea milkwort, sea arrow grass, sea wormwood and sea couch grass. In areas close by are pyramidal and southern marsh orchids—beautiful.

Spring cinquefoil, greater knapweed and dog rose are found on the turf reaching the shingled shoreline. Where the path comes alongside a huddle of pines, which each year become wearier from the relentless exposure to the winds, a birdworld fracas greets my arrival. Two carrion crows are back to harass the pair of kestrels which have made use of the old nest of another crow pair, perhaps theirs, and have raised their young here; these are also shrilling, accompanying the noisy confrontation between parents and antagonists.

Farther on at the mouth of the estuary the strip of sand dunes holds clumps of hound's tongue.

On the lower saltmarsh the roosting curlews and gulls become suddenly agitated and then rise into the air— a seal swims alongside the bank, having taken advantage of the high spring tide.

Halcyon, mesmeric days unfold for our delight—every moment of every day begs to be committed to memory.

> . . . he had been visited by rapture, by a sense of life's sheer beauty and joy and goodness so strong as to be almost mystical. . . he had been reduced to tears by an apprehension of beauty and mortality commingled.

'Hard Facts' – Howard Spring

I am, first and foremost, a nature-lover, not an expert. To me nature is a living poem, to be read quietly and alone. And how often I must borrow my emotions from the poets. Pastures can be emblazoned with the millions of golden chalices of buttercups or with that "wee modest crimson-tipped flow'r", in such density as "an immeasurable constellation", a fallen Milky Way at our feet . . .

> Daisies, those pearled Arcturi of the earth,
> The constellated flower that never sets.

Shelley

These common intrinsic, yet special, wildflowers, beloved by poets and children alike, have understandably accumulated much lore over the centuries. Their attraction ever holds firm to me.

A profusion of appealing wild flowers bloom in chosen quarters of our cascading hedgerows. Twining anti-clockwise through supporting herbage and twigs, the hedge bindweed and the introduced great bindweed often achieve blanketing growth. The best means of separating the two species is by examining the bracts, those of the latter being much bigger, covering the sepals of the (likewise) bigger flower. Insects are, of course, fond of these plants.

As well as on disturbed land, given the opportunity the (yellow) ragwort will appear in any position of the hedgebank—much to the annoyance of farmers, who pull it up at every opportunity. Cattle normally avoid browsing on this plant, but if it is taken (in sufficient quantity) the milk yield becomes tainted. The farmers' main concern, though, is if it is compressed in bales of hay, because here it could react and become toxic. During childhood rambles on farmland it was ritualistic for me to ward off members of a herd from the vicinity of ragwort. To this day I have a certain reservation for

The Footpath Way: 'Where'er we tread, 'tis haunted, holy ground.'
Byron

An unsullied verdant landscape

Above : *Carrion crow's nest in 'climbable' oak*

Below : *Blackbird's nest*

Left : *Foxglove spire.*
The discovery of this goliath
certainly made the diarist's day.

Right : *Navelwort or pennywort.*
With its whitish flower spikes it
is commonly seen on (shaded)
walls and stone-banks.

Above : *Sedge warbler proclaiming its territory*

Below : *Common frog in kitchen garden*

Right : *Holly tree of prodigious girth. It is frequently used by deer for rubbing their itchy hides*

Left : *Himalayan balsam. Its flowers offer a soft sweet scent along many a riverbank*

Above : *A primrose-studded North Devon lane*

Below : *A Lundy backdrop*

Above :   *Fulmars, stiff-winged 'little albatrosses' nest along our indented coastline*

Below :   *Mute swans in romantic mood*

this plant—even though the caterpillars of cinnabar moths make short shrift of it.

Greater stitchwort is essentially a hedgerow plant and this is the time its existence is marked with a show of white, five-petalled flowers. The damp base of some hedgebanks may harbour the cuckoo flower or lady's smock. Bird's foot trefoil sometimes anchors to a dry mid-section spot of this rich habitat and flourishes, normally though it is found on level grassy areas. Cleavers, or goosegrass, in flower . . .

The hedge woundwort is quickly identified by small, dark maroon florets. Lesser hawkbit is verge-hugging where most of the dandelion family frequent: all are very attractive to bees. Both the pink flowered common mallow—with its rough haired stalks—and the ox-eye daisy, are sometimes seen in the hedgerow also, but more often inhabit rail and roadway embankments.

One of my favourites from way back is the black knapweed, found along the verges of many of our country roads, lanes and footpaths, and a magnetic force to all manner of insects, not least the *Lepidoptera*, the most beautiful order, drawn by the purple flower-head to the rich wells of nectar therein.

In evaporated pools and streamlets and the cattle or sheep bare-trodden ground of gateways into fields the greater, or rat's tail, plantain and the redshank, or redleg, *Polygonum persicaria* take hold.

A cheap but wholesome salad from the brook.

From 'The Task', Book I – *Cowper*

Minor roads with slow-running water channels, small ponds, streams and rills can become overwhelmed with watercress. When I was a child no particular attention was accorded to the selection of these plants to supplement the salad bowl.

Nowadays though, with the 'accepted' standard use of chemical sprays throughout agriculture—sprays that often drift from the place of application—and the contamination perpetrated by an unimaginable increase in numbers of motor vehicles it is a different picture altogether.

You cannot kill time without injuring eternity.

Thoreau

The deceit of 'progress': the madness of a commercialized synthetic world . . .

The coppery flowers of common sorrel are a familiar sight on many a hedgerow. The vinegary leaves are, nonetheless, edible. Later the three-sided seed-discs will be in prominent display.

During June the garden hedge-bank of my late childhood home was cloaked with green alkanet, a picture, but one which at some stage was invariably erased by the use of a paring hook. My father—being the latest (and last) in the line of an (utilitarian) agricultural lineage—was instinctively compelled to keep nature in order. Numerous bees and other insects visit the smallish blue white-eyed flowers of these tall rough-haired plants of the borage family. I enjoyed their company, however brief.

Many years have elapsed since the day when, walking in a field of clover and jubilation, I caught sight of my first clouded yellow butterfly. As is usually the case with this species it must have been a year when 'irruption' had taken place. But although I have returned there in subsequent years, its kind has not, to my knowledge, graced that particular locality again.

Irruption is the term to describe a sudden influx of non-endemic species driven either by extraordinary favourable or adverse conditions (of an environmental or climatic nature) during the breeding season in their land of origin, whereon 'erupting' becomes necessary for survival. Now in my middle age I have, to date, seen this beautiful butterfly in only five of the many summers I have had the good fortune to savour.

Some additions to my moth list for the year to date are eyed and poplar hawkmoth—and I have seen both in close proximity on the same night (R. L. E. Ford wrote that a male Eyed Hawk moth will sometimes mate with a female Poplar Hawk moth). Hummingbird hawkmoth, swallowtail moth—a large and impressive species—silver Y, common heath, cream-spot tiger, figure of eighty, bloodvein, cream wave and sallow kitten.

By dint of my grandfather's large fruit and vegetable garden I was, at an early age, acquainted with gooseberry bush infestation of ('loopers' or 'inch measurers') caterpillar colonies of the magpie moth. Nowadays they do not appear anywhere as common, doubtless the cause for this, as usual, lies with the wretched use of chemical sprays . . .

The lushness of the countryside is being voraciously yet 'invisibly' attacked by an inestimable army of insect larvae that are superbly camouflaged to match their particular surrounding. Countless 'loopers', the larvae of several moth species, feed among the trees and herbage alongside 'conventional' caterpillars (with a full set of prolegs.) Yet so luxuriant is the prevailing general growth, that in all but a few cases, little of this deleterious onslaught shows significantly.

The damage wrought by the larvae of the large white butterfly can be another matter. Batches of eggs are deposited by this species on cabbage and other brassica plants. Nasturtiums are also a target. Later, left to their own devices, the caterpillars strip the leaves skeletal, much to the consternation of gardeners and horticulturists. (If handled the caterpillars may, in defence, release from their mouthparts a greenish substance).

But however successful in attaining full growth, many of these caterpillars, liveried in green and black with yellow stripes, will fail to reach the adult (imago) stage. Parasitism— mother nature's complex engineering against overpopulation—has the final say in their destiny.

One of the braconid flies, *Apanteles glomeratus,* a tiny black insect, seeks out the 'cabbage white' caterpillar. On selecting an individual it will insert eggs, maybe over a hundred, into it. These eggs form the grubs which hatch and feed on mine host. At a given time these vacate the devoured quarters and pupate in small yellow-silk cocoons alongside the shrivelled skin of the victim.

An ichneumon fly does likewise, the female of the species adeptly manipulating the specialised ovipositor to pierce through the skin of the caterpillar and deposit its eggs. When, believing itself to be ready for pupation, the 'full-fed' caterpillar leaves the food-plant, the grubs spill out of their (former) living disguise, a common enough sight on many an undersill or garden wall near to the cabbage plot or nasturtium bed.

83

The large white caterpillar that has avoided the attentions of parasitic flies and is now pupating still runs a real risk of meeting the executioner's gaze. At the eleventh hour and with pupation complete the not yet hardened exterior of the chrysalid can be attacked by a chalcid fly that implants eggs from which another platoon of grubs emerge to eat their unspeakable lunch.

From the order *Hymenoptera* there are many families and innumerable species of parasitic flies—preying on insects such as the gall wasps that are parasites in their own right; the combinations are intricate and manifold. Yet, with clear bright colouring, and long flickering delicate antennae and slender bodies they all prove compelling to study. Who could suspect their motivations?

When I reflect on the constant battle-ground that is the natural world and the insect world particularly, my thoughts time and again are on Francis Burrows' lines:

NATURE'S FRUITFULNESS

This summer on our yard-wall there does swing
A groundsel-bush from one seed last year sown.
A burnet moth, sun-awakened in the Spring,
Flew out and laid its hundred eggs thereon.
An hundred seeds each blossom on it gives,
An hundred caterpillars eats its leaves.
Its plumed seeds scattered by the wind now fall
Into our yard on water and on stone.
Here too the caterpillars over blown
Gyrate and starve, for few can climb the wall.
Next year again there will be one of both:
One bush of groundsel and one burnet moth.

The poet mistook the cinnabar caterpillars for those of the burnet moth, a similar-looking species. We must accept that in the 1930s he didn't have the benefit now gifted us of a plethora of excellent reference books. That aside it provides a stark plain lesson on nature's strict domain which humankind perilously disregards . . .

Nature needs to be let alone. Free to her own devices, she cleans her own house, knows no wastage, makes no biological mistakes. She solves for herself the problem which men are still finding insoluble—that of a balanced economy. What alone has for ever upset it is this man-child of hers himself, this Homo sapiens, in particular the white man, the builder and the destroyer.

The Road of a Naturalist   *Donald Culross Peattie*

More and more butterflies.

The much respected field maple holds its horizontally winged fruit. In the hedgerow of the next field a tartar maple is classified—the leaf veins impressed at the underside. In the often visited woodland, herb bennett and slender sedge, and a canopy now leaf-filled, the beech leaves percolating the sunlight . . .

Relaxing in the garden I look skywards into the blueness above me and contemplate. Contemplate the fragility of our earth system with its mere three miles of life-giving atmosphere. Contemplate earth's protective magnetic field (largely) deflecting the radiation bombardment instrumented by solar cyclones from our sun that is big enough to absorb a million planets the size of ours.

And our solar system on the outer spiral arm of the Milky Way, 3,000 light years from the galactic centre and in company with a million stars in this area of the galaxy. My thoughts are distracted by a faint sound and I watch the eggshell (a house sparrow's) lightly roll along the garden path as if to prompt me to say Earth, our Earth a living gem, set in the immensity of space . . . lonely, yet vibrant.

On the 21st we reach the longest day: to tell of all there is to see would be impossible, each moment of the long daylight has a hundred tales to tell, a hundred delights to savour.

At 6.30am, after a stormy night, a 'sunburst' . . .

Dryad's saddle (dryad meaning a wood nymph) is a bracket fungus that lends a certain quality to dead or dying tree stumps or stoles (or mutes, as they are known in Devon). It is, however, deemed to be injurious to unfelled trees because it taps into the living tissue. Look for the barely perceptible 'puff-clouds' of the millions of spore as these are released into the breathless air of woodlands.

If not every village then every parish has at least one long-relinquished stone quarry close by. Decades have passed since sturdy blocks extracted from these centuries-old sites were used in the building of farms and farmyards, cottages, lanes and hedgebanks, leaving a scarred void in the side of a steep rise. But nature, all conquering nature, has now stealthily re-colonised her former territory, installing new forms of flora and fauna to the gouged, man-made setting.

Close to the village where my formative years were spent, the quarry was ever visited with a deal of expectancy. Near the top of the sharply rising horseshoe field that encloses the quarry is a spring. Needless to say the floor of this quarry is throughout the year almost completely submerged in water, five or six feet at its deepest point. It is home to a pair of moorhens which have stoically nested here, with both success and failure (egg collectors and predators sometimes strike) for a run of years.

The platform incubation nest is built in the half-submerged branches of an alder tree that had, when a sapling, lost its hold at the rim of the quarry face and toppled fortuitously into the soft mud at the water's edge. Its roots repaired a less than tenuous hold on life and made good, in time its branches reaching out laterally into the centre of the pond. Moorhens are said to use 'nursery-nests'.

Understandably, the perimeter of the quarry has been fenced off to protect livestock; the ungrazed land inside quickly reverted to its natural state with hawthorn, sloe and oak taking full advantage. Here, amongst others, wood pigeon and magpie nest.

Entering the quarry from the lower side, along a long forgotten overgrown path, one is suddenly in the open and *vis-à-vis* with towering rock. This rockface, by virtue of the spilling water, becomes during very cold winters an 'iceberg' as columns of thick icicles are formed and extend from summit to base. Entering the quarry this way on one occasion my attention was diverted by a sudden harsh "chack" from the vicinity of an oak on the other side. *Lanius cristatus*, a red-backed shrike, was perched on a thick branch of the oak, clutching the remains of a young blue tit which it was shredding with falcon-like bill. I was open-mouthed with incredulity at the rare spectacle.

My usual observatory was the highest point of the quarry, where the perimeter of trees was broken, and only grass and a few gorse bushes impeded the process of inching forward to the edge to view the moorhens' nest below. Despite my supreme caution, the 'sentry bird' would sometimes be in a position to immediately spot my presence, warning the brooding mate, which dived off the nest and into the murky water.

But my eye automatically follows the 'bow-waves' formed by the submerged bird aiming for the bolt-hole at the side of the pond. On scrambling ashore to make off into the undergrowth, a harsh scolding starts combining with the rhythmic jerking of tail to display a conspicuous white underside. This pair were truly of the wild state, untrusting of man and so much more secretive than the 'urban conditioned' type one associates with parks, etc.

Here I have spent many golden hours, absorbed in watching the moorhens, with the warmth of the sun on my back, and accompanied from time to time from either side with several other bird species going about their business in the trees and bushes at the rim. And usually a willow warbler or two, those will-o-the wisps that flit quietly about the branches, catching small insects and uttering soft 'hoo-eets'.

The only pond in the district that used to be frequented by little grebes—dip-chicks to us locals—is now filled in and is a hard standing for agricultural machinery.

Around from the sheltered bay and on the exposed wind-blasted path some 70 metres directly above the sea-swell I have scanned the rocky ledges with binoculars and telescope to pick out the breeding guillemots, razorbills, kittiwakes and gulls that have been in occupancy for a number of weeks. I decide for once to get a new perspective of the breeding colonies. Lunging through the steeply-sloped oak wood and then out onto the scree and bracken-covered open land near the cliff-top, I descend on a path more befitting a goat than the biped who, on turning to look back up the promontory to the figures of colleagues hovering more than a cathedral's height above, is suddenly light-headed, assailed by the sudden awareness of vulnerability.

The path levels out and ends on an earth-capped 'reef' and I gladly accept the silent invitation to sit and survey and accustomise. Fulmars, our 'little albatrosses', glide past parading both an acquiescent and inquiring countenance. And I find myself on a level with the seabirds at their cliff-ledge nest sites. There are perpetual eddies of activity as the parent guillemots and razorbills arrive and depart on whirring, oar-like wings to skim the undulating blue-green surface—in contrast to the considered strokes and soaring glides of the sharp-eyed herring and black-backed gulls that glorify flight. I am in a magical setting that etches on the soul. . . .

The prickly sow-thistle, relished by one's pet rabbits of yore, grows in various, usually disturbed locations: the milky sap it contains earning it the Devonian label 'milky-dashel'. Silverweed enjoys dampish grassland, whereas a close cousin, spring cinquefoil, will thrive on very dry patches of ground—the very habitat enjoyed by the pineapple mayweed, of which I have an enduring fondness, an attachment that harks back to those long ago pre-school days when it grew in the lane and farmyard where, as my father worked nearby, I played. A time recalled instantly by the scent which I had first discovered all those years ago by plucking a few sprigs and my hands becoming aromatised. Being somewhat of a purist where nature is concerned, and deriding the past practice of introducing foreign flora and fauna, it came as some surprise to read that my plant was brought (depending on the reference book used) from either Northeast Asia or North America.

Dog rose blossom. Wild strawberry fruit. Bittersweet flowering. I have discovered three areas where pink purslane grows—three quite different (dampish) sites: the shaded ground by the old barn; a copse—which is sheeted pink, so prolific are the plants here; and along a short stretch of hedgerow. A lovely little flower, introduced way back from North America. Creeping jenny can also be found in a similar woodland aspect. Inwards from the border of a mixed woodland, dame's violet flourishes. Vigorous bunches of common comfrey can never be overlooked along their wayside habitat.

The scarlet pimpernel :

> When hollow winds begin to blow,
> The clouds look black, the glass is low,
>
> Closed is the pink-eyed pimpernel.

Dr Jenner

. . . is a beautiful, much overlooked 'weed'—a weed rightly defined as being a delightful plant merely appearing where the gardener thinks it shouldn't. At stream-pool margins the water forget-me-not flowers, and farther back from the water's edge ragged robin. Lustrous banded agrion and blue-tailed damselflies are also here and a joy. Along the stream's tree-lined bank the elderberry puts out its fragrant creamy blossom, attracting the attentions of a wide variety of insects.

TO THE OBSERVER—UNBOUNDED PAGEANTRY

On nettle-patches may be found the click beetle *Agriotes lineatus*, the nettle weevil *Phyllobius pomaceus* and, inside the rolled up leaves fastened with silk threads, the caterpillars of the mother-of-pearl moth. Whenever nettles are given the freedom to thrive insects take full advantage; caterpillar colonies of small tortoiseshell, peacock and the 'woolly bears'—preyed on by the cuckoo, the only bird capable of digesting it—of the garden tiger moth. Note the fascinating group behaviour of the peacock caterpillars when danger is deemed to be at hand: there is instant petrification by all, held for a good minute or longer, until one, deciding the coast is clear, recommences feeding, whereon the remainder quickly follow suit.

A prime example in the *Coleoptera* (beetle) order is the common cockchafer or maybug. Active in large numbers at night, it often strikes windows in its strong flight. However it is a common enough sight during the daytime, as it dawdles about. The pectinate (comb-like) antennae and the hard, light-brown elytra (forewing) are a striking feature, along with tipped abdomen of course. It seems every flowerhead of cow parsley holds the soldier and sailor beetle, *Cantharis livida*,

89

an orange-brown species which, when it isn't coupling, awaits the arrival of small insect prey.

In the splendid larch plantation I have noticed numerous goldcrests' nests strung under the branches. Afforestation has benefited this, our smallest bird, even though, generally, conifer plantations cannot match the wildlife sustained in the deciduous woods. . . But for all that, the 'thinned out' coniferous habitat appeals to me, and I am always pleased to tread the 'needle laid paths' and inhale that distinct resinous aroma. Buzzards will nest in the mature trees. I watch as small birds mob incessantly a tawny owl roosting in a pine—it eventually succumbs to its tormentors and moves off. This is also a good place to find the strikingly coloured horntail or wood wasp.

My maternal grandparents' house stood on the edge of a plantation and one afternoon a horntail somehow managed to enter the living room, to dash itself noisily against the window. At the age of seven I was awe-struck by this first sighting. The female is the larger of the sexes and is a wasp coloured black and yellow, with long ovipositor for which it is named. It is harmless in the adult stage but the grubs which tunnel inside the wood are very damaging to the timber. During the evenings, at the same house, sitting out in the porch was a recreation enlivened by the pipistrelle bats that swooped in just over the head, to attend the young that were ensconced between slate and planking. Later, curled up in bed, the screech owl's nightly ululation was awaited with pleasure.

From the family of flies *Empididae* comes *Hilara maura*, a species which on many past occasions caused me to pursue it in order to determine 'that small airborne puzzling configuration' . . . This is due to the fact that the male of this otherwise regular looking fly often cradles an insect prey—shrouded in the silk administered from the front tarsi, or feet—as a (tempting) offering to any would-be partner when in flight around hedgerow or pasture. Should a female be enticed by this, mating takes place in flight as she feeds. A puzzling sight indeed, this triple-formed flying insect, to the uninitiated.

I once retrieved from the lawn an adult house martin that was strait-jacketed from beak to wingtip by a thick spider's web. How this came about I can only guess, but after spending several minutes extricating the resigned bird it was free, and left my hand with the same and was out of sight in the blink of an eye. Now is the time for these birds—Richard Jefferies descriptively called them the white-rumped eave-swallows—to concentrate on building their mud-pellet-fashioned nests. These are domed-shaped and attached to a wall under the eaves of farm buildings and human dwellings of both town and country; well over two thousand pellets are ferried to form each new home.

Nowadays those who appreciate the special charm of these birds but do not possess a nesting colony on their property install replicated plastic nests to encourage them to patronize a new site.

Two years ago a novice pair of 'eave-swallows' began to fasten mud pellets under the eaves at the front of my house but alas, only a 'foundation' was ever made, the enterprise being curtailed at an early stage. Perhaps the 'pair?' were having a practice run? Interesting to watch the martins gather at the rim of a muddy pool, collect and shape the pliable mud into pellets and return eagerly to the nesting site. Henry Thoreau recorded the following habit of martins on terra firma.

> And as he spake, his wings would now and then
> Spread as he meant to fly, then close again.

From 'Walden'

An open patch of moistened earth—by a water course or puddled farmyard or gateway perhaps—is critical for the nest-building operation of house martins. A friend told me of someone who assists these hirundines when baking hot days coincide with mud-pellet gathering. Near his house, if the heat of the day threatens to dry out the site of extraction, the obliging gentleman arms himself with a watering-can and promptly dampens the ground, enabling the industrious activity to continue close at hand to the colony. A pleasing, considerate gesture indeed.

Years ago a particular colony of house martins were observed at a farmyard I visited once only. Here the gable-end of the stone barn held an unbroken line of nests from eaves level to roof apex and I remember thinking what a marvellous time one could have had with a cine camera—video camera now of course—filming the perpetual eye-blurring comings and goings of the parent birds as they strove to satisfy the appetites of the ravenous nestlings.

In my early teens treasured times were spent in observation along a particular hedgerow. This had been allowed to broaden out a couple of strides or more from its original line—a parallel thicket of intermixed interlocking of shrubs and bramble that afforded the perfect habitat for a wealth of life. Here, on stooping, I would back into a narrow, naturally formed tunnel and melt into the mass, 'better to become associated with the activity of nature's toilers'.

Directly below, some mammal, probably a bank vole, would be heard gnawing at roots: then the humblest of tremors as it scurried along a subterranean passage. The soporific sound of grasshoppers, bees and flies: floating butterflies: of birds on branches and sunlight on leaves. And always, like the cloud-shadow that drifted across the field, a timelessness that imbued the soul. Just yards away partridges, oblivious to my being. At dusk nibbling, scampering rabbits; and moths a-stirring in the still air. I felt privileged beyond measure.

Walking alongside this species-rich hedgerow one fine June afternoon, my attention was drawn to the excited 'churring' of a common whitethroat with its crown feathers raised, and dipping in and out of a blackthorn bush. Knowing the clever and courageous ploys adopted by many nesting birds to divert a threatening presence, I began a careful search, now bravely faced by both parents, a mere arm's length away. My search was quickly over, a flimsy structure of woven dried grasses, attached to a blackthorn sapling, contained four small, dark-downed nestlings.

The discovery achieved, I retreated far enough to allow the whitethroat pair to return without alarm, and the feeding restarted in earnest. I watched each of the birds return several times, green caterpillars dangling from their bills, before continuing on my way in a state of headiness to match that of a discoverer of some place or thing quite exotic.

A cousin of the whitethroat (and lesser whitethroat) is the blackcap. Perhaps a little more retiring than the former, though its choice of habitat—the entangled undergrowth of woodland margins and so forth—contributes much to this judgement. Often one catches a glimpse of a feeding bird as it makes a delayed succession of 'hops' to advance along the bramble-tops. When an intruder is confronted its sharp "tacktack" alarm notes—renting the quietude—are as unmistakable as this warbler's appearance.

In a woodland clearing a mile from my first whitethroat's nest I have found the equally frail constructions of blackcaps, old and new, strung in the brambles which grow freely here. The blackcap is a songbird of some rank, with a rich and melodious voice, known in the past as the mock nightingale and, in the north of the country (where the latter is absent), the 'northern nightingale'. Additional—and vernacular—names are jackstraws in Somerset and haybirds in Northamptonshire, due to its use of dried grasses in nest construction. Yes, the largely quiet sylvan haunts of the blackcap are ideal for the solitary soul.

Many birds, regardless of the result in rearing the first brood, are now repeating the strenuous devotion to procreation. One spring I found three robin's nests, one of which was in a decaying tree stump on the side of a hedge, and here in due course two broods were successfully raised.

June, therefore, is the month when untold numbers of fledglings vacate cleverly concealed nests to gamble with fate in the extensive, and hostile, world all about them.

An amusing incident occurred one day when I was walking in 'rushy plat' (the haunt of snipe at the opposite end of the yearly cycle). There was movement in the spray of the lowest bough of one of the hazels lining the hedge—quickly I crouched low to the ground. Some thirty strides away and partially hidden behind a clump of the numerous rushes where the spring water surfaced I began watching six young wrens tightly in line along the slender perch which dipped and swayed in protest. The fledglings were being encouraged to fly by the flustering parent.

But it appeared to be a one-sided affair as none of the siblings seemed in the least bit interested in taking to the air, until the wand buckled unexpectedly. Then there was a feeble perfunctory fluttering of wings as six young wrens plummeted unceremoniously into the fall-breaking nettle-bed. No harm resulted from the incident, however: a few days later I again met up with the family, two fields distant from the 'skydiving show'. Sitting on a stile for a brief rest and to look about, I suddenly found myself flanked on both sides by the whole wren family, not the least concerned by my presence, and now adept fliers one and all.

The tree-creeper brood have also ventured from the nest and much noise ensues from the moss-covered beech bough. Here more interest is shown in obtaining food from the parent than in their unexplored woodland kingdom.

Hedge trimmings, left where they have fallen, help to conceal the ground nest of the partridge. Such is the camouflage of the nest that only the rising of the sitting bird—a heart-stopping moment for sure—betrays its whereabouts. And what a delight it is, to see a dozen or more porcelain-smooth, olive eggs, nestling warmly together.

On a summer's day in my eleventh year on this wonderful earth my birdwatching life truly began. By the hedgeside I lay in the grassy-hollow (formed many years previously by the hedger—doubtless wielding his long-handled Devon shovel when repairing a gap by using the soil and grass clods from the field) and with a quiet ardent elation, watched a spotted flycatcher.

I can visualize it now, perched on an old lead water pump standing in the field corner that supplied the cattle once quartered in the now dilapidated stone and cob barn. In typical manner it would rise and pursue a fly, covering its evasive moves with agile twists and turns of its own and usually ending with a snap, signalling a successful mission. More often than not an immediate return to the pump followed, and, after a wipe of the bill, a sharp eye out for the next passing insect.

. . . Again in those early years, on one of the oft indulged days playing lawn tennis at the Vicarage. After one of those inevitable mis-struck volleys I trotted off, voluntarily, to retrieve the 'skied' ball from a deeply shaded corner under towering pine trees and its infill of evergreen laurels. Stooping under a laurel's base of fanning limbs I hunted the missing projectile.

Presently it was found: backing out and straightening up I was arrested by a spectrum beam which parted the gloom. At the spinney's sunladen edge an upper casement had accepted the brief entry of refracted light. The beam's shallowly angled fall reached the tip of the bare lateral branch—that lay toward the one inner clearing—and the profile of a spotted flycatcher thereon was bathed with a physical, saint-like aura. A composition fit to adorn any of the stained glass windows of the church. A fine, fine example of nature—random imperious nature without artifice, composing in a chance moment a scene that, as W.H. Davies poetised "I shall never recapture, this side the tomb".

For I tell you, that many prophets and kings have desired
to see those things which ye see, and have not seen them;
and to hear those things which ye hear,
and have not heard them
St Luke

JULY

So I will build my altar in the fields,
And the blue sky my fretted dome shall be,
And the sweet fragrance that the wild flower yields
Shall be the incense I will yield to Thee.

Coleridge

n every respect a cornfield daubed with the vivid scarlet of common poppies is a rare canvas to behold. Each flower lasts but two days, when the 'pepper-pot' seed capsules form. Poppy seeds can remain dormant for a hundred years and still germinate.

When the present-day madness of herbicide spraying with toxic chemicals is seen to be just that, and ceases (always to haunt our folly-filled past), let us wish that a goodly number of inert seeds of legions of displaced wildflowers will also germinate and the plants reappear, like botanical phoenixes, and cloak the countryside as in the pre-mechanized days of yore.

Reclining on a grassy knoll at the field border, in the shade cast by the oak alongside, my eyes skim the sun-beaten cornfield. The shimmering heat, and the timbre of distant yellowhammer notes befit my langour. Then, a rustling movement from the barley's edge keens my senses. A hen pheasant, with raised leg momentarily poised, steps into the anxious open. She weighs my presence with fixed curiosity and I, in turn, attempt to gain her confidence with a 'glassy stare' . . .

Waysides and hedgerows are swaddled with herbage: hedge parsley (in the past known as Queen Ann's lace) and also the fine delicate fool's parsley.

Note that the fresh new plants of teasel are only prickly on the underside midrib of the leaves. Tall, stiff-stalked plants— ribbed melilot, weld and vervain are now in flower along the wayside and on waste ground, the vervain having rather incongruous, yet appealing, small lilac-coloured flowers.

Close by, plants of bristly ox-tongue, which before flowering would almost pass as cacti; self-heal by the woodland path and, but for a rest and a sandwich and a flask cup of tea back in the half-light, under the trees, a solitary bastard balm would have been missed.

In the small quarry, growing alongside honesty and dame's violet an impressive bear's breeches—all three are garden plants, but who or what introduced them here? Spear thistle is also present.

Betony and common toadflax are rich in number and often grow in close proximity. Wood sage aplenty, also red bartsia; field woundwort, and in some cornfields, field pansy—almost certainly some scentless mayweed.

Common valerian now crowned in pappus; yarrow, white and pink; hedge bedstraw and hogweed. Perennial sow-thistle, tall. Spindleberries green. Dogwood berries green and yellow. Alder fruit lime-green.

Half a mile from the coastline I find wild madder threading a hedgerow. At first sight I assume it to be cleavers, but one touch of the rough stems censured this notion.

On the quiet country roadside a songthrush's stone anvil, with dark-lipped banded snail shells scattered around it.

A freak of weather. An increasing spate of tornadoes in the U.S.A. are seen as a side-effect of global warming. In the early 1960s I remember my father telling me that on the farm he had been working that day, near Exmoor, practically a whole field of baled hay had been swept up and deposited elsewhere by a whirlwind.

Combine harvesters are at work and, as always, I stand and look on in awe. The scene could be light years from the days of horse-drawn binders, let alone the scythers of old or a sickle clasped by biblical Ruth. (And the men shall come singing from the fields, for they have provided for their own . . .)

Last summer I found swallows' nests in a number of sites—two on ledges outside of buildings, one in the canopy over the loading bay of a factory (where the incubating bird was observed during the night changing position over the eggs just as in the daytime).

Contrastingly, the second 'open' site was under the thatched eaves of a cob-and-stone cottage. The lych gates of two local churches are also providing a safe harbour for the swallow pairs. Nests are found inside a number of the more usual setting of barn and outbuilding.

On a beam supporting the galvanized roof of a 'lean-to' abutting the cob-and-stone barn, a swallow's nest held four nestlings. I watched the four jostle vigorously to gain an advantage whenever the adults approached with a catch of insects. Other broods in the village have already taken to the air; the 'kissing' in the skies is a parent feeding one of its young.

Before a particular industrial estate had been fully developed the land earmarked for this was left in a state of limbo and transformed into a lush meadow, brimful with wildflowers and insects.

A pair of skylarks and wheatears continued to breed on the land. However these birds were ousted when new buildings were erected on the site. In the following spring a single wheatear came back and (in despair?) flew inside the warehouse now occupying its former territory as if to seek confirmation that none of it remained. When and where will it end?

4th July. 21:45 hrs. All creatures black. Dusk, and the short stretch of river which earlier twinkled in the sunshine now glides almost invisible. Above a swift passes in level straight flight. Next a flock of jackdaws noisily travel out from the hillside to halt over the near bank, and then mysteriously veer back whence they came. A cormorant then heads in the same direction as did the swift some few minutes earlier. Shortly after three large bats—long-eared or serotine?—hawk high above the river and part of the narrow field alongside: the hostilities from clouds of biting midges assure the watcher of abundant catches for them this night.

Pixiated. A friend's recent telling of hedgehogs racing in a circle on his lawn one night brought back to me the time I witnessed just such a happening. I was nine years of age and shortly after dusk—it must have been a weekend, or during school holidays, for otherwise bedtime was normally 7.30 p.m.—I was looking out of the window onto the garden, with apple trees and in a far corner saw shadowy movement in the form of a spinning-wheel. "Ah, that'll be the pixies," retorted my smiling parents when I asked what could possibly be moving so . . .

Near the seashore are frosted orache, prickly saltwort, musk mallow, tutsan. . . Along the cliff-tops English stonecrop and thyme supersede thrift and bladder campion. Here also is lady's bedstraw. Montbretia, a hybrid perennial garden iris, grows wild and in lengthy patches in several locations, not least by watercourses. The deep orange flowers now open, enticing large numbers of bumble and honey bees.

Himalayan balsam can grow exceedingly tall in areas where light is restricted, i.e. under alders and other trees that form canopies along the riverbank. I have seen plants towering to twelve feet.

This introduced species can hardly be confused with any other, even those of the same genus—touch-me-not, orange and small balsams. The fleshy stems are most often pink-red. The flowers have a pleasing, 'soft' perfume that wafts on the late summer air. It has certainly found a niche unoccupied by native flora—the bare sandy patches that punctuate the edges of most rivers.

Because of its height certain stands have to be scythed annually to allow fishermen a free sweep with their fly-lines. The seed pouches are a source of wonder: on ripening these are sprung and, upon contact, hurl their contents several feet inland or out onto the river. To me this plant has become synonymous with untold quiet hours alongside the rolling waters.

The resident reed bunting and that tuneful summer visitor the sedge warbler both enjoy a similar habitat and, although our reedbed areas are distinctly few and far between (and dwindling), the reed bunting isn't as reliant on such habitat as the latter. The reed-beds of the ox-bow lake I have known and visited throughout my life are a sedge warbler stronghold but—like the water rail—their fortunes here in North Devon are mixed, and far from assured.

The dunnock, *Prunella modularis*, is normally unobtrusive in its ways, except, that is, during the mating season, whereupon the males boldly take to the hedgetops to sing with no little spirit. The parasitic cuckoo knows full well that *Prunella* makes a good foster parent and probably keeps an eye on the nest of grass, hair, wool and moss to time the depositing of her egg among the bona fide, but doomed, clutch. I found my first cuckoo egg nestled innocuously in turquoise-blue.

In an oak woodland the thin-stemmed common cow-wheat peeks up at the hovering pied flycatcher and the flame-tailed redstart dallies about the glade, which resounds to the 'linen-tearing' of argumentative jays. In open country yet within quick reach of tall concealing grasses one may be lucky enough to witness fox cubs gambolling in the midday sun. These pretty youngsters play like puppies, and wag their tails similarly when the vixen appears to satisfy herself that all is well with her family. On a sunny afternoon I have watched an adult fox prance stiff-legged—like a Spanish horse in a dressage event—in the tall grass attempting to catch what I could only assume to have been beetles, or some small mammal.

With their quarry plenteous those mustelids the stoat and weasel are in fine fettle, although even the briefest glance of their sinuous movements during hunting activity is witnessed infrequently. Who has seen a hunting pack of weasels? Not I
. . .

A weasel was seen slinking along under the bottom horizontal plank on the opposite side of the gap in the hedge. But, just at the point of disappearing again behind the recommencing hedgerow it caught my advance, some twenty paces back in the field and, in one movement, turned full circle and rose up on its haunches to give me a scrutinous eye before continuing on its way.

"The countenance of the teeming world of insects is a mesmeric swirl of intrigue."

The insect world vastly outnumbers all other living organisms; perhaps 90% of all creatures are insects, with doubtless tens of thousands awaiting discovery—if, in the meantime, certain habitats remain in existence. And insect adaptation stretches the boundaries of one's imagination. Metamorphoses is the stronghold of the *Lepidoptera*, i.e. butterflies (*Rhopalocera*—referring to clubbed antennae) and moths (*Heterocera*—other forms of antennae).

Since my schoolboy days and beyond I kept caterpillars. My sons continued the tradition during their early years. Sometimes even now the compulsion is overpowering and a jar appears in the study, filled with nettle- or grass-stripping larvae. I always took the commonest species to raise in my glass case—garden tiger, small tortoiseshell, peacock, cinnabar, small and large whites. Occasionally a full-fed privet or elephant hawk moth would be found wandering away from a garden shrub and be 'rescued' by being popped into a jar filled with soil or cotton wool, wherein pupation took place within a day or two. To be privy to the change from caterpillar to chrysalis or, much later, to witness a perfect butterfly emerge from it, still fills me with the same wonder I felt in the heady days of my youth.

The brightly coloured caterpillars of the lackey moth, the blue side stripes prominent, enjoy sunshine, and those that are full-grown are regularly seen stretched out across a hawthorn or bramble leaf or whatever the food-plant happens to be. The younger caterpillars sun themselves over their silken tents where they rest and moult. I learnt recently that caterpillar colonies spin these tents not solely for their protection from predators but also to maintain warmth during uncongenial days, little greenhouses in fact, enabling the inmates to remain mobile to venture out, in short bursts, to feed.

A surprising 'find' during the school holidays many years ago was a small group of five caterpillars of the 'swallow tail butterfly' on burdock leaves (not their usual food-plant) at a certain locality on the edge of Exmoor. I wrote to the producer—Winwood Reade—of an inspirational BBC nature programme of the day called *Out of Doors* telling him about the discovery. In his courteous reply he suggested that maybe numbers of this species had been blown across from the continent and bred. Many years were to elapse before it dawned on me that the caterpillars had in fact been those of the mullein moth, a shameful realisation.

Bramble blossom of softest pink attracts many butterflies. Meadow browns and ringlets—and gatekeepers, so abundant as to outnumber both. In complete contrast to these is the attractive and mettlesome small copper. From a combined resting place and vantage point on some flower or grass head it launches into a territorial defence against any encroaching fellow, and almost always a larger, *Lepidoptera*, its speed immediately overwhelming and shepherding away the latter. This chase is sometimes swiftly curtailed on the appearance of another unwitting intruder, which is given the same treatment.

The large skipper, too, often interrupts, with brief play, the considerably more sedate flight of some larger butterfly. Broad-headed, thick bodied, short-winged dynamos with prominent eyes, the skippers, family *Hesperiidae*, are—dingy skipper apart perhaps—anomalous to the butterfly kingdom. On rainy or cool days this species, like the majority of insects, will be in a state of torpor. Without difficulty and (more importantly) damage, the handling of these 'miniature combat planes' is then easily achieved, transferring from plant to palm of the hand for a close and novel inspection.

Where the bee sucks . . .

In grass fields the red and white clovers are visited by innumerable honey bees, genus *Apis*, and bumble bees, genus *Bombus*, reaping a rich harvest of nectar with their sheathed tongues, while hind tibiae bulge with pollen to be transferred into the larval cells back at the nests. But farming practices such as the rooting out of hedgerows, where *Bombus* seek nesting quarters, and the application of chemical sprays, have destroyed untold numbers of these irreplaceable agents of floral fertilization. To add to the honey bees' catalogue of woes, the *varroe jacobsonii* mite (which has spread across Europe, from its Asian origins, and into Britain) is striking hard.

The group ethos inherent in the apis hive is skilfully portrayed in Maurice Maeterlinck's title *The Life of the Bee*. Many schools have lessons on bee-keeping, a pursuit that remains as popular as ever. It has been estimated that over a million flower heads are visited in order to make a pound of honey, 'the liquid essence of summer'. And the workers may travel an outward distance of four miles to reach plants in bloom.

The keeping of bees is like the directing of sunbeams

H Thoreau

Cuckoo bees, genus *Psithyrus*, are mimics of bumble bees but do not possess the latter's pollen-carrying 'basket' on the hind tibiae. But no matter, they enter the *Bombus* nests, kill the resident queens and leave their own eggs for the workers to rear.

Potter wasps are eminently watchable in their industry. In multitudinous number, larvae of a certain sawfly species have totally stripped my garden salix. Unlike the caterpillars of the *Lepidoptera* these fellows do not have claspers on the tail end and have the habit of flicking their back half into the air.

Scorpionflies are locally common and I love to watch them go about their business along the shaded hedgerows which they tend to inhabit. Although the male bears a dangerous-looking 'scorpion tail' the raised abdomen tip is completely harmless. Delving into tall, geniculate herbage growing at the foot of the hedgerows one can discover the fascinating 'subterranean' world of insects and 'mini-beasts', maybe ground beetles, weevils, millipedes, bugs and rove beetles such as the instantly recognizable devil's coach-horse.

I can never pass by a shield bug, they fascinate me. I have seen maybe half a dozen or so members of this substantial family. *Elasmucha grisea*, the parent bug, is so named because it cares not only for its eggs—just as the pied shield bug does—but for the young as well, when they have hatched. Wonderful stuff.

An insect flies hither and thither along the hedgebank then hangs over bramble blossom, and I see it is a longhorn beetle. Beetles in flight are compelling images.

The summer of '96 was a notable hummingbird hawkmoth year (migrants come here from the south of France) and I registered several along the coast, one on Lundy and others inland. I have observed the astonishing swiftness of flight of these remarkable moths as an individual hurtles back and forth along the face of a cutting near the cliff-side. Incredible things. (The food-plant of the caterpillars is bedstraw, commonly found along the coastal margins.)

A latent interest in moths was re-ignited some four years ago when my employment changed and I became a night worker. Drawn, through half-open windows and doors, to fluorescent lighting came a goodly range of species.

Not one moth is uninteresting. From clothes moth to hawk-moth all have individual qualities that are exciting. The micro moths need to be studied using a magnifying glass to appreciate fully their design of dazzling metallic colours: the many-plume moth and larger white plume moth cannot fail to impress with their 'feathered' wings.

Note also the fascinating and contrasting resting attitudes of moths. Most rest with the wings pressed flat against the surface on which they are attached, or held along the line of the body, fore-wing over hind, in varying degrees of compactness. (The poplar hawk moth is a notable exception to the rule, exposing the hindwings ahead of the fore.) Only a very small number hold their wings closed together over the body like butterflies. The plume moth forms a crucifix with its 'narrowed' outstretched wings. Another micro moth, *Ypsolophus harpella*, rests with head touching the resting surface with abdomen raised into the air. Legs and antennae are also held in differing poses, depending on the species.

Successive hatches of moths. During late spring into mid-summer the family *Arctiidae* gives us three very similar, and attractive (but aren't all moths attractive?) species. The white ermine and muslin moths normally emerge before the buff ermine. These species have a soft 'furry coat' on the head and thorax. Later in the month we may meet the white satin moth of the family *Lymantriidae* to which belongs the yellow-tail moth that, apart from this feature, is also a white ('hairy') species.

July 17th. National Moth Day.

Some of the host of moths to be seen now are cream-spot tiger, ghost moth, drinker, clouded border, the clay, mullein, barred hook-tip, early thorn (second generation), yellow shell, brown line bright-eye, green silver lines, scarce silver lines (its beautiful green colouring fades if exposed too long to a lighted room), the miller, the common footman and willow beauty. The willow beauty is a lively insect and its feathery (plumose) antenna seems to be constantly in action. I love moths, even though I have only seen a fraction of the two thousand five hundred macro (meaning larger) and micro (smaller) species found in the British Isles—the micros outnumbering the former. These are separated into about 50 families, compared to the nine of butterflies.

The country road—on really hot days its tarmac bubbling to form a lunar landscape in miniature—sees the occasional cries-crossing of a number of small mammals, and caterpillars. Resolutely lolloping along could be a full grown and lengthy fox and/or drinker moth caterpillar searching out a grass stalk firm enough to bear its weight. (Often when cycling the local country roads I have to make any number of stops, to dismount and pick up caterpillars of these two species and place safely in the hedge or verge away from danger). When a suitable plant is found the cocoon is spun and pupation takes place. From time to time when I have handled these handsome caterpillars—in drinker moths dark, yellow spotted and hairy, with thick tufts near head and tail—I have regretted doing so because my fingers suffer urtication, a painful stinging-nettle effect which persists for hours. (The loose hairs on the browntail moth caterpillars are notorious for causing this condition).

Several species of (nocturnal) moths can be disturbed during daytime rambles, either from brushing past branches or herbage, or by traversing recently cut grassfields. The narrow-winged large white plume rests in the hedgerow during the daylight hours, and here also, perhaps shaken off some higher sprig of hawthorn, is the light emerald moth. In the hayfields innumerable small, light-coloured grass moths are found, usually resting head downwards on stalks of grass, and glancing away from almost every stride. The light arch, much bigger, is also present here, and around the borders of fields where nettle patches flourish, the snout moths are awakened by gently brushing the leafage with one's foot. Also, amongst the bracken, the brown silverline can be startled into life.

In the garden the diurnal cinnabar moth is a common and attractive subject. In looks and habits this species (family *Arctiidae*) seems closely related to the burnet moths (family *Zygaenidae*) but obviously there are more dissimilarities than matching ones—hence the difference in family grouping. However both species are poisonous and, even though predation would be easy owing to their weak flight, they are left well alone. Feeding on ragwort and groundsel the familiar orange and black banded caterpillars of the cinnabar store up alkaloid poisons, while those of the burnets ingest cyanide derivatives from bird's foot trefoil. These toxins they can carry through the metamorphic stages into adulthood.

In the preparation of vegetables one may find that the heart of a cabbage has been eaten away by the green caterpillar *in situ*. This is the larva of the garden pebble moth (family *Pyralidae*), a minor pest. During summertime, to enjoy the wonderment of the insect tribes one needn't go farther than even the most modest of gardens, where there is almost certain to be some activity which will draw the eye. There bumble-bees and hover-flies can be watched effortlessly—with an ever-widening appreciation of 'what-they-are-about'. The violet ground beetle briskly clambers over nodules of soil. Buddleia bushes encrust with butterflies during the day and draw the cabbage moth, among others, at night. But also before our eyes the eight-legged arachnids portray the melodrama of life, checking the infiltrating insect numbers.

Following skilful means of ensnarement the prey succumbs to a stab from the pair of poisonous spider fangs and, when the resulting paralysis takes effect, its body fluids siphoned off. The orb-web spinning spiders are greatly admired for their symmetrical designs, and rightly so. But there are numerous other types catching their meals by different and no less efficient methods. Hunting spiders, such as the crab spiders *Thomisidae*, are wonderfully camouflaged, enabling them to lie in wait, without detection, on plants and flower-heads for unsuspecting prey. The zebra spider is one of the jumping spiders and *Pisaura mirabilis* is commonly found on the tops of nettle leaves, where it is often espied in a sun-bathing pose.

The early evening sky was a plane of marble.

In its membranous swirling flight a bat suddenly twists and stalls, to net another in an endless booty of moths. Evidence of such captures are revealed the following morning when the wings of species such as large yellow underwing, bufftip and old lady are left lying on the ground. Estimates have been made of the average nightly captures of moths by a single bat but I dread to consider the magnitude lost to the 'weight of combustive traffic along our roadways.'

The pipistrelle, our smallest bat, is said to feed mainly on midges. The pipistrelle will squeeze through the smallest of openings in order to roost. I once found one secreted behind a tile of the gable-end cladding on a bungalow—apparently a common occurrence. When I see a small bat hawking for insects I have always assumed it to be *Pipistrellus pipistrellus*, but now I'm not so sure as there are other species of 'flitter-mouse'. So, I must now endeavour to honour these amazing, highly evolved mammals that use ultrasonic squeals to navigate and hunt with sublime precision, in even the darkest of nights, by becoming *au fait* to their identity.

It is well into dusk as I walk along the estuary footpath. A barn owl on silent-fanning wings heads straight towards me and I quickly see it is deep in concentration, scanning the ground to both port and starboard for signs of movement. In the split-second we meet its talons almost rake my cap, then the hunter is past and quickly lost in the gloom, oblivious to a brush with an inwardly smiling homo sapiens.

Following the sunset the forest ride overlooking the glade gradually transforms from the scintillating haunt of insects, flowers and birds into a silent, dark-shrouded arena framed by the silhouettes of trees—unnerving. (Throughout mankind's history night has been linked with fear, mystery and superstition. In the modern world, at nightfall, we rarely find ourselves far from the aid of artificial light—landworker and poacher aside).

And novel it is to experience the profundity that darkened stillness remote from habitation can bring. I am here with a group led by the forest ranger to listen to and, hopefully, to see nightjars. Apart from our guide we were unprepared for the swarming crepuscular midges that ambushed us the instant we arrived. Focusing on the biting, discomforting 'clouds' that engulfed us, the first 'churring' that broached the gloom was greeted with tepid enthusiasm. It had been stated that the calling bird serenaded its brooding mate by using a number of perches that encircled the 'nest'. Tonight, however, this would not be corroborated, for the 'churrer' unexpectedly flew along the ride toward us, veering over the tops of the conifers and away without so much as a whip-crack. Just two of us witnessed the flight—the midges had subjugated most everyone's interest that night.

26th. Sitting with a friend in his cottage garden we are surrounded by a 'squeaking-wheelbarrow' of sound from a family of wrens. Then a youngster pitches briefly on his knee before flying to the strawberry bed.

All iridescence, a starling bills water from my garden bird-bath.

27th A family party of four ravens circle four church towers high over the village. The youngsters that were seen at the nest at the end of April are now truly world-wise.

Sailing out to Lundy for the annual viewing of the puffin colony we see a gannet or three home in on the vessel and, keeping aft with the noisy gulls, move alongside when scraps of food are thrown into the air. Low in the wave-troughs small parties of shearwaters challenge the attentions of the sea-watchers. An hour or so each year spotting the pelagic species is truly magical.

Two negatives: on the south Devon coast I have watched numbers of gannets plunge-diving, but not here off North Devon. And, although they sometimes show themselves around the island, and off the coastal bays, I have yet to meet a basking shark.

On the other hand, a pod of porpoises in the bay, oh yes.

AUGUST

Fairest of months, ripe summer's Queen
The hey-day of the year
With robes that gleam with sunny sheen
Sweet August doth appear!

R. Combe Miller

o me August, heat-soaked August, like no other, is the month when sunlight—conjuring a plenitude of active life—and shade, beseeching inactivity, rub shoulders. Out in the open we can enter or leave these contrasting settings with manifest ease.

The limit of natural resurgence is August's cast:

The feeling of fullness and pause, the saturation of life
with its own achievement, spreads its persuasive influence
to every detail of leaf-spray, flower and ripening seed.

E. L. Grant Watson

The little river bids me leave the brightness of the meadow valley path to inspect its shaded course between the alders. On the underside of the fallen tree-trunk lying across both banks I watch the water-reflected light dancing chimerical. Then, seconds later, a bolt of blue over this natural bridge, as the halcyon, catching the angled light to glisten its back deep-blue, disappears into the cavernous distance.

Motes in the lanes of the sun . . .

In 'aimless benignity' I cycle along the high-banked, sun-filled country road—ahead lies a wooded dell and maundering stream. I am drawn to dismount, to leave the road and, in the

109

shadowy light, follow a short path to the stream. The cool soothing water flows over jet stones, sedimentary in origin. I cross the stream in two short strides by stepping on those stones (dry, and so reverting to the true colour of grey.) that break the surface, and climb over the gate alongside.

Ahead of the widely spaced trees growing at the foot of the steeply rising rough pasture there is brilliant sunlight. I am propelled to this. It is almost boyhood revisited—a time far-off (to which I shall shortly relate)—for the slope is new territory to me and inundated with butterflies, and other insects, among the wildflowers. Ringlets, meadow browns, gatekeepers, fritillaries, peacocks, small heaths, common blues and skippers; rank grasses, trefoil, bramble, ox-eye daisy, field scabious. Here a golden hour thus spent:

> Where every prospect pleases, and only man is vile . . .

Where the skilful efforts of forestry workers have claimed innumerable rows of pine trees for the awaiting sawmills, a whole new generation has been likewise planted in their place. Until this fresh stock develops to a suppressive degree, the etiolate undergrowth rears into verdant life across the vacated ground. Diminutive yet tenacious roots are unleashed to spurt across the barren tracts till, suddenly, herbage swathes the undulating slopes.

Taller than all except the evening primrose—and clambering bramble—is the rosebay willowherb, daubing the whole scene in crimson flame. To such plants are drawn a wide, rich range of iridescent insects and, alluding to the tropics, the strong, forthright flight of the silver-washed fritillary is a sight one always relishes.

I remember the first time I saw this butterfly. I was twelve years old, and was walking in a former plash-meadow being drained by the process—at that time—of hand-laying innumerable clay field-pipes. Slowly I was surveying the ground vegetation for caterpillars and butterflies. As I neared the brambled hedge a silver-washed fritillary rose from the blossom and I, aghast at the size of my 'new' butterfly, engaged in immediate pursuit. It swept majestically over the rush-clumped ground while I, in my determination to identify it by gaining a closer view, floundered over the clayey clods forming ramparts to the trenches over which I leapt.

I never succeeded in achieving another view, however: the winged beauty dipped over the hedge and was gone. Of course it had to have been this species. But you can imagine the scenario from an onlooker's perspective: before him a demented soul who firstly inched along with eyes fixed to the ground and then, away in frantic pursuit, of what? Since those early formative years one can become almost blasé about spotting the species that had been the cause of such initial excitement. (That said, throughout life one is always discovering new species with an elation equal to that of the earlier days.)

Cycling along the country road where it dips down to the bridge over the stream, I am flanked on my right by a conifer plantation wherein a small team of foresters are skilfully thinning-out. Behind me as I proceed to climb the short but steep hill, a chainsawed tree rents the air with crackles and hisses as it careens through the branch-screened path to earth. This, and the reverberation along the valley, reprise last night's thunderstorm . . .

From the gateway at the bend of the hill I look across the steep field which runs down to the stream bordering the plantation where the forestry work is being carried out. Thistledown ascends nymphean and multiple into the breathless air from a large patch of thistles. This instantly prompts me to reflect on the poem *Beleagured Cities* by F. L. Lucas—the 'battering thistle-down.'

Two large and impressive moths abroad just now are red underwing and oak eggar. Aside from the large hawkmoths, there cannot be many species bigger than the red underwing. Attracted to the light in the room as it passes the window it enters and quickly rests: a gentle prod and it flits, exotic and 'butterfly-light', its hindwings fully on display. A privileged sight.

Photographing the specimen I discover brushes on the middle legs. According to my reference book this indicates that the individual is male: the brushes are thought to produce pheromones—a volatile scent—to attract the females of the species.

The oak eggar moths in the area seem to be the sub-species found mainly on moorland in the north of England and Scotland, but also here on our own Devonshire moorlands. My book says the female has a wingspan of over 3 inches (90 mm) and the dead specimen I retrieved from the road measured just that.

With consummate ease the swallow flashes across the flight path of a young house martin making its languid way on fluttery wingbeats.

4th August. On Exmoor I notice that both whortleberry and rowan fruits give hint of the opening bloom that is a turn towards ripeness. Tormentil seen on many a roadside grass bank and on the moor itself.

In ancient woodland, marked as often as not by the yellow flowers of cow-wheat, holly trees of great age and girth may sometimes be found. There is a wood on the Somerset side of Exmoor's borderland with North Devon where such holly trees exist. One in particular, alongside a bridleway, is a mammoth $4^1/2$ metres ($14^1/2$ feet) in circumference. Deer seem to favour it for rubbing against, as a small area of the bole is worn silky-smooth. Further evidence, if needed, is the several strands of hair on the ground directly below.

Wednesday 11th August 1999. Eleven minutes past eleven a.m. and the village is mantled in 'dimmit' light. Eleven starlings are perched on the battlements of the church tower facing south. Whenever these birds are settled here almost always they face outwards to the west, today however they face towards a great natural phenomenon, a full solar eclipse. (Astronomers and scientists will be busy collating data on the sun's corona amongst other things—to help measure the solar storms which graduate through an eleven year cycle: solar storms which have a direct effect on earth life.).

I remember the partial solar eclipse of 1957. This must have occurred shortly after midday, for at the time I was enjoying a cooked meal at the Village Hall with my peers from the Primary school. (To this day pupils likewise daily vacate the school and walk up through the village for their 'canteen' meal).

From the middle of August a pair of siskins pay regular visits to the peanut-holder in my garden.

Month by month the Big Dipper bobs and tilts in the ethereal ocean. Soon Cassiopeia will be climbing . . . Look for the 'summer triangle' as described by Patrick Moore. Vega, the brightest star of summer, is directly overhead; Deneb is in the north-east and Altair in the south-east. Along some deep hedgebanks the numerous 'hammocks' of spiders are thickly peppered with bracken spores. High up in the dappled sun-light snails cling to sycamore leaves.

At 6 am at the weir I watch, stock-still, a family of dippers. In turn they go under water to feed or gambol at the rim, and fly to perch on exposed rocks in the shallows below the fall. A kingfisher is perched on an alder branch nearby. "The secret of all living creatures is quiet . . ."

Birds of passage? At the beach near the waterline a flock of over two hundred ringed plover with fifty or so dunlin and thirty-odd sanderling: a good summertime sighting.

Access to transport when one is older allows one to range farther afield than in earlier years when one's parish (one's 'narrow sphere') was one's world. Now I look on the whole of North Devon as being my parish. And within a twenty-minute drive I can reach a certain woodland border where it is very likely that half a dozen or more silver-washed fritillaries are flying. And just last year when I was visiting an aunt, a silver-washed fritillary swept in from the garden to inspect her con-servatory: with doors ajar conservatories are prone to 'trap' many an exploring species of insect, and quite often birds as well.

Soon after entomology had taken its hold on me, at eleven years of age, and I had acquainted myself with many of the commonest *Lepidoptera*, I happened upon my very own 'butterfly meadow'. To reach this I had to walk along the tractor-rutted lane wending its way through the conifer plantation. (At the bottom of the plantation ran a stream accompanied by a footpath where the fetid stinkhorns grew). At the time the phalanx of trees—later to be thinned, as is the way of forestry—permitted very little light, and on the lane's final twist the bright vista of oak-posted gateway was most effecting.

Leaning on the gate, I squinted into the sudden brightness. In the seconds that followed I was aware that several butterflies were flitting over the rough grasses and sward of that sun-kissed slope. I entered the meadow with expectations high. Here indeed were some wonderful (and to me new) species. Six-spot burnets seemed to be everywhere, and their yellow cocoons were strung from countless dried grass stalks. Large skipper, meadow brown and small copper also abounded. And the hummingbird hawk moth was indeed a revelation as it burst onto the scene, pausing here and there to circle a choice flower head, and on uncoiling its long proboscis, sipping the nectar.

Anchored to a patch of scentless mayweed was a colony of marbled whites, wonderful—an especially admired species; and nearby birdsfoot trefoil drew all the common blues from thereabouts. Throughout my examination of the slope the field grasshoppers, those sun-loving 'vectors of stridulation', relayed an orchestration of rasping song to celebrate my *Satyridae, Lycaenidae, Sphingidae*, etc.

At the bottom of the slope the stream emerged from the dim-lit wood out into the open sunlight. Here those 'aerial torpedoes', the hawker dragonflies, patrolled, and the dainty damselflies flittered up quickly to re-alight on figwort, fool's watercress and rush. In the backwater, pond skaters twirled and jigged on the surface film and, inverted beneath, the water boatman oared toward the drowning fly.

After a subsequent visit to the meadow-slope that season I was climbing the gate to head back home when, with great excitement, I glimpsed another completely new species— albeit imprinted in my head from book study—a comma butterfly. It had been resting on the gate post's angled top but was now away to settle on a bramble bush down along the hedge. I made towards it. But again it was up and away. Its desultory and unpredictable course gave me little encouragement: but then it pitched on another bramble leaf and I quietly approached, closer and closer. Again it fluttered up, circled around behind me and to my utter disbelief came to rest on my shoulder. What an introduction!

Alas, revisiting this meadow in later years I discovered it

had been 'improved'—in other words ploughed and seeded in rye-grass, that most spiritless of plants. Now my butterfly meadow exists only in my memory. Ah, the numbers of rich meadows that have been lost to the sowing of a single, alien strain of grass. Did not our 'old' breeds of cattle thrive by grazing the rich grasslands of former times? The warped demands of productivity are manipulating the breeding and feeding processes to a peak that is indefensibly unnatural.

> Wisdom is oft-times nearer when we stoop
> Than when we soar.

The cuckoo will soon slip from these shores, the adults and fostered young taking their separate ways.

THE CUCKOO

(*Old West Country Version*)

In March he sits on his perch,
In April he tunes his bell,
In May he sings all day,
In June he changes tune,
In July away he fly,
In August go he must.

And the swifts too! About now they might be seen suspended high above the church tower, for them a siesta. In a 1982 copy of *Bird Life*, the magazine of the Young Ornithologists' Club, Chris Mead wrote:

> The oldest British-ringed swift is over 16 years old. Since swifts are in flight all the time, except for the short time on the nest in summer, this bird has probably flown a distance of over eight million kilometres. This is the same as ten return trips to the moon or 100 days in Concorde at full speed—all achieved by a bird weighing about 40 gm.

As summer progresses there is increasing paucity of bird tunes. Call-notes have replaced full song: even these sounds are few and far between. (Many of our resident—and summer visiting—birds have raised up to three broods and are now into moult). There is of course the "tak tak" of stonechat, "pee pee pee" of nuthatch and the cries from a new and demonstrative generation of buzzard. Likewise, in the late evening and onward to dawn the "ke-wick" and hoots of the parent tawny owls. Though the wistful robin is soon to be heard.

From conifer plantation, broad-leafed woodland and oft-ivied hedgerow tree, the soporific cooing of wood pigeons puts the seal on indolent high summer. Harvesting begins in earnest—fields of barley, wheat or oats, and in recent times rapeseed oil and flax; and the 'settlements' of many small lives—harvest mice and other rodents and smaller mammals—duly obliterated.

A red deer hind had a long stay in the oatfield, judging by the 'terrestrial' corncircle.

One afternoon during the previous month, I spent several very frustrating minutes vainly attempting to pinpoint the unusual call emanating from a field corner. Eventually the 'thrown' "quic quic-ic" call of a quail was traced to the adjacent flax-field—now reaped—a short distance in from the gateway. Recalling memories of grasshopper warbler encounters.

There are something like fifty species of ant in Britain. On a particular south-sloping field there are more than two dozen hummocks, eighteen inches tall, the nests of meadow ants. Most of the tireless yellow-tinted workers will be patrolling far from their nests seeking-out the taller, aphid-infested plants along the hedgerows. When found, the scale-bodied aphids will be hauled back to the colony and farmed for their honey-dew secretions.

Go to the ant, though slugged;
consider her ways, and be wise.

Proverbs. VI. 6

THE ANTS

What wonder strikes the curious, while he views
The black ant's city, by a rotten tree,
Or woodland bank! In ignorance we muse:
Pausing, annoyed; we know not what we see,
Such government and thought there seem to be;
Some looking on, and urging some to toil,
Dragging their loads of bent-stalks slavishly:
And what's more wonderful, when big loads foil
One ant or two to carry quickly, then
A swarm flock round to help their fellow-men.
Surely they speak a language whisperingly,
Too fine for us to hear; and sure their ways
Prove they have kings and laws, and that they be
Deformed remnants of the Fairy-days.

John Clare

At any time now, meadow ants and the commoner black ants will become embroiled in their respective nuptial flights. This swarming is indicated by the wheeling gulls, and other birds, that snap almost randomly at the multitudinous 'winged males' seeking a liaison with the few besieged queens. Soon pathways are a-crawl with exhausted and disorientated consorts which have played a role in the continuation of the species, and now face an inevitable end: starvation. The queens, however, return to terra firma, rid themselves of their wings and prepare to form new colonies.

In cattle-haunted meadows the ginger-yellow dung-flies rise up from the pats in swarms, quickly re-alighting as one passes. Cleg and horse flies attack the cattle relentlessly and the poor creatures often make for hedgebank or tree trunk to rub themselves free of their tormentors. Wall brown butterflies like nothing better than the bare patches of soil which cattle have created.

There is a second hatch now of the saffron-coloured brimstone.

The small white deposits singly its skittle-shaped eggs on the leaves of my nasturtium.

With much the same courtship behaviour as other butterflies a female dark green fritillary flickers her wings shallowly as she alights on a fern at the side of a brightly lit plantation ride, the male right alongside. The following day I observe a pair of wall browns performing the same courtship on the bare earth under a gate. Presently the male, seeming to lose interest, flies off into the field, but soon returns to continue a-wooing.

Newly hatched butterflies visiting knapweed and the like are as good an example as you will get to illustrate the creative beauty, both in design and colour, of nature. Comma, small tortoiseshell, peacock, red admiral, painted lady and the various 'blues', even the 'whites', display before us.

The exuberance of procreation is unleashed as the butterfly that moves along the 'stepping stones' of flower-heads suddenly responds to the presence of another of its kind; but is it courtship or rivalry? Whatever the situation it triggers an instantaneous vertical spiral that rapidly hoists the pair up and up and out of sight.

The attractive noontide fly, denoted by the orange colouring at the base of the wings, enjoys nothing better than to rest in full sunlight on a tree trunk or wall.

Purple hairstreaks are seen swarming around the crown of the oak, such an important tree. Over a hundred species of moth larvae feed on, or are closely associated with, this venerable plant in some way. Eight species of footman feed on the lichens growing on it, goat and leopard moth on the wood, the yellow-legged clearwing on the underside of the bark and common fanfoot on the dead leaves below. Although perhaps it is now out of print, see if your library can get you *The Oak* by Ralph Whitlock.

Of course not only is the oak a great dormitory for insects such as moths and butterflies, but also a wide range of birds and animals; and for epiphytic plants such as common polypody. Historically its valuable timber, used for shipbuilding and mining, meant large areas have been felled.

Everyone should plant an oak.

Among the moths to look for are swallow prominent, willow beauty, smoky wainscot—a species which, if touched, will have you believing it is dead—wainscot grass-veneer, dark swordgrass (an immigrant), August thorn, purple thorn, common white-wave. Attractive grey dagger caterpillars can be spotted on a variety of trees and shrubs.

On wasteland prickly and least lettuce, with mugwort.

The old hollowed out ash bole on the hedgebank gives the appearance of an ancient Greek actor's (giant) mask for some tragic play.

Along a country roadside ditch watercress thrives, with flowers on top and seed pods down the side. From a different family, fool's watercress is growing (prostrate) in close company. Burnet saxifrage and redshank also.

Corn parsley, golden-rod, perennial sow-thistle and great bindweed. Angelica flowers later than most of the *Umbelliferae* and is readily distinguished owing to its purplish stems. It grows in damp places. The pink and white umbels of hogweed hold many small insects and its leaves are being 'mined'. One or two giant hogweed plants can be found annually in one coastal locality—this, an introduced species from SW Asia, reaches a prodigious height. Hemlock water dropwort is showing the dry cylindrical fruit. Meadow vetchling has black pods and tufted vetch, brown ones. Search the bare ground around gateways for knotgrass and pineapple mayweed.

Guelder rose, a striking bush in late spring, is eye-catching again with bright red fruit.

Green berries of bryony, orange berries of honeysuckle, scarlet rosehips, elderberries green (but stalks red). The spadices of lords and ladies topple!

Eyebright, a parasitic plant, is seen to be plentiful along the trail. Laurel showing green berries. Tassels from sweet chestnut.

In the town the exquisite perfume from the blossom of the Indian bean tree, and London plane showing fruit.

Growing in front of the brambles on the top of the bank near the estuary are field scabious and sawwort, the latter being visited by an occasional butterfly or two. Below, on the rockface, is rock samphire (once gathered by brave lads as a treat for older folk). At the top of the tideline, sea wormwood.

Back in the late 1950s and during a summertime visit to the beach I saw—or did I bend my imagination into seeing?—

a chough. Chances are it was a jackdaw flying along the clifftop but, I will never know for certain. Oh to see one now in such surroundings. And to think that in the mid-1800s choughs haunted much of our North Devon coastline: on Lundy they were numerous.

Sneezewort in the damp areas by rills and hedgerows. Common fleabane and ragwort; haresfoot clover; yellow rattle, on the burrows and along a short stretch of country roadside way inland, now seeded. Teasel heads changing hue; traveller's joy in flower. Soapwort has formed an extensive range along one roadside hedge.

Meadowsweet is the favourite wildflower of many a country person—including this one—and its fragrance, from flowers that cream the hedgerows, is with us throughout the summer months.

I cannot recall chicory growing elsewhere than along two stretches of country roadside.

G. K. Chesterton wrote that "the rolling English drunkard made the rolling English road"; an Australian friend visiting recently fully agreed with him. Being used to the wide, straight and usually level roads of his homeland, he here found that he 'drove for miles but never got very far'. Without doubt, our maze of hedgerows, a defining quality.

Last year's fuscous/black 'cotton spools' of reedmace are pronounced. Buckshorn plantain leaves turn purple; sea lavender has brought the moorland scene to the estuary. Hidden in the saltmarsh's lush green of *Spartina* (Townsend's cord-grass) are curlew, teal, grey heron, little egret, greenshank and redshank. Eel grass and glasswort here.

A member of the finch family not often seen in this area is the crossbill. Once, when cycling leisurely along a country road flanked on the right by mature towering larches, I was startled when suddenly several cones hit the tarmac in front of me. Instinctively looking up into the trees from which these came I caught sight of a small flock of birds but could not make a positive identification. Tossing the bicycle into the hedge and clambering up over the machine in one swift movement I managed to get a closer glimpse. "Crossbills!" I muttered incredulously. Next moment the birds had taken flight into the depths of the plantation, leaving me transfixed for several moments.

Birds are re-grouping. Swallows and house martins have been congregating for several weeks. A few wood warblers may be seen with some willow warblers or chiffchaffs and titmice. At the end of summer the titmouse tribe often band together to form quite sizeable flocks. Comprised of blue, coal, marsh, and long-tailed, they sift through the woodland canopy in a procession urged ever onwards with "see, see, sees". Peculiarly I have often encountered families of long-tailed tits near woodland streams merrily feeding and calling as they advance through the hazel and alder. And a pleasing portraiture they make.

For a time the mistle thrushes are to be seen in small flocks. Are they the broods of a breeding pair? Or maybe two neighbouring families have banded for mutual protection? Whatever the case these truly wild thrushes, flying at height with power and speed about the open countryside will soon disperse to a more recognised solitary or paired-up existence: a contrasting existence from its sartorial, and oft suburbia-frequenting, cousin the song thrush.

In comparison to times past nature's larder of wild fruits is hardly tapped by human hands these days. For some the harvesting of hazel nuts ('nits', to use the vernacular), whortleberries and the like were a precious commodity. During the first quarter of the century organised parties from the towns were annually brought out onto the moor by horse and carriage or charabanc. And in his evocative biography of his grandfather's brother—*DICKY SLADER, The Exmoor Pedlar-Poet*—J. M. Slader described how . . .

> During the summers, when the hot sun blazed down on the parched moorland, Dicky would often be out on Fyldon Common picking whortleberries. His 'territory', he said, was from Moles Chamber to Sandyway Cross. "The best whorts in Devon. Pick 'em in me own 'at so ems mus' be clean," he would say.

(The air is thick with larksong there). From his cottage at Molland Cross Dicky would walk to Barnstaple, Lynton, Bampton and 'neighbouring' South Molton to sell his 'nits', 'whorts', blackberries, sloes, fresh-laid eggs—"I know they's fresh, I laid 'em meself"—and a variety of wares. He was the last great countryman of North Devon.

And ah, the high moors cloaked in purple by the heather: memories of deep cleft valleys with streams a-glinting and studded with hawthorn trees: of sundew, ring ouzel, whinchat and pipit. Emperor moths; harrier, merlin and buzzard. And the hobby, catching on the wing not only dragonflies and other large and manoeuvrable insects but also such aerial experts as house martins, swallows and swifts. Soon the hobby will be journeying south to the Mediterranean and beyond.

Summer walks arm in arm with autumn.

Autumn

t this time transience is law. Described by E. L. Grant Watson as 'a decay of jelly', an abscission layer of dead cells forms between the base of the petiole, or leaf stalk, and the twig to which it is attached. Soon the breezes or winds will snatch the jettisoned organs and strew the ground with a variety of shapes and colours. Since time immemorial the process of decomposition, by plant and animal agents, has recycled the nutrient properties of the leaves back into the life-supporting soil. A never-changing pattern . . .

Although many plants have, throughout summertime, been setting seeds, now fructescence peaks.

Blackberry bushes laden with glistening fruit are a magnet for blackbird and songthrush, and the lovely dormouse. In the oaks the colourful jays reap the acorns, tugging at the green fruit before these ripen and fall freely to the ground— some of the crop will be stored by the birds and used according to their needs. Likewise, hazel nuts are garnered by the grey squirrels, to be buried in caches here and there. Dreys of squirrels, set in the stout forks of trees, are a familiar sight even though these are covered with beech twigs and leaves.

A sunny autumn such as that of 1997 meant that the beech leaves were late in displaying a burnished red-copper, both on the majestic trees and along the miles of centuries-old trained hedgerows: the 'fall' was correspondingly late.

Swallows and martins gathering along the telegraph wires give the appearance of notes of music on a score: daily, at eventime, squadrons of Canada geese home-in to the upper estuary from distant feeding grounds, many performing an exuberant wing-tilting semi-roll action—one wing then the other—before descent; rising levels of fresh water assist the migratory fish; colourful fungi; the worn wings of insects; the first frosts.

Gamebirds again flee the beaters and guns: fox and deer blend with the rich-brown hues of brackened field, woodland and moor.

At autumn's end the countryside itself seems culled in preparation for the incursion of winter. Hollow plant-stalks and leaves, fallen twigs, branches and bark—the residuum from the fullness of summer—together with inorganic rocks and stones even the dwellings of man doubles as shelter and armour for the small proportion of creatures that sidestep winter's telling adversities.

> In the soft light of an autumnal day,
> When Summer gathers up her robes of glory,
> And like a dream of beauty glides away.
>
> S. H. Whitman

AUTUMN

> Harvest moon, lambent shortening days,
> champagne-crisp air, migration and
> expendable life!

The "season of mists and mellow fruitfulness" arrives in name only, with barely perceived changes: weeks may pass before nature's weary face is apparent. At the beginning of September the worn-wings of butterflies are more often the first and only indicator to the time of year.

The sky deepens. From the gradual declining altitude of the sun, the refracted light glitters the wing-tips and undersides of birds that, for their protection, gather into flocks to see out the trials ahead.

Daylight hours shorten. Nights become clear and chill.

As daytime temperatures inexorably fall, sap no longer rises: there is an accelerating withdrawal of plant and insect life.

Be it from a scientific or layman's angle, whatever our understanding of how the colours of autumn are formed, the response is universal: a woodland canvas or a single tree in bold colourful expiration, our senses are delighted.

> The autumn of the beautiful is beautiful.
>
> (from the Latin) *Francis Bacon*

The autumn leaves of trees undergo a process known as senescence, where the leaf tissue begins to die. Chlorophyll is the dominant (green) pigment of several—carotenoids and anthocyanins making up the list—found in leaves and is vital to photosynthesis. Although photosynthesis continues awhile the progressively lower temperatures reduce the movement of sugar around the tree, and a change in the physiology of the plant occurs. This results in the chlorophyll breaking down, and no longer masking the plant's pigments: these can reveal their own splendidly rich colours.

The beauty of the autumn is proverbial, and autumn has been called the "Sabbath of the year". There seems to be a pause; the ripening glory of the summer has reached its full splendour; winter's decay has not yet set in; a restful Sabbath calm pervades all Nature; a short respite before the silence and harshness of winter is upon us.

William Coles Finch

SEPTEMBER

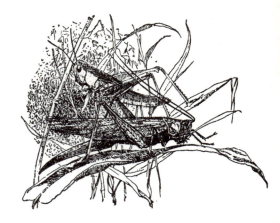

he melliferous days of summer recede and the last one or two days of August, on into the first of September, allude to autumn, the morning air laced with sharpness, with wraiths of mists and dew-laden fields.

> In brisk wind of September
> The heavy-headed fruits
> Shake upon their bending boughs
> And drop from their shoots;
> Some glow golden in the sun,
> Some show green and streaked,
> Some set forth a purple bloom,
> Some blush rosy-cheeked.

Christina Rossetti

The untold industry of innumerable insects has pollinated a rich diversity of plant life. This extensive toil has transformed our waysides into a banqueting hall of brightly coloured fruits and fertile seedlings of wildflower, bush and tree. And contingent to this fertility is dispersal—in all manner of ways—from aeons of evolutionary adaptation.

Waning nature spawns a bounteous store.

The guelder rose is garb'd and ensplendoured with large umbels of rich-red fruit. Black berries grace the tutsan. Fleshy red berries of honeysuckle glisten in the dew-fresh morning. Spiky seedheads of burdock are designed to affix onto any passing mammal, being thereby distributed further afield. Agrimony also similarly developed, its 'miniature bells' worthy of inspection.

August saw the rowan bearing a great weight of red berries; blackberries also were appearing in number. That said, 'tis September that sees the full ornamentation of our hedgerows and waysides with glistening fruits.

Clusters of ash 'keys' dangle from the branches and sycamore seedless spin to the life-supplying soil below. The spiky husks of sweet and horse chestnut expand in response to the developing much-sought fruits within. The conkers are treasure: polished mahogany enwrapped in white satin. The game of 'conkers' is still played by youngsters; one village holds an annual competition.

Beechmast has been spilling from the trees for some weeks and throughout the lean times ahead will sustain a host of wildlife species, finches particularly. Hazel showing catkins. The hazel-nut kernels, developing inside the hardening protective outer shell, will be sought by squirrel and nuthatch alike.

Acorns are revealing their expanding shapes in the oaks, while the branches of elderberry, hawthorn and rowan still remain laden with their distinctive fruits. The 'hips' of dog rose also compete for the attentions of birds and small mammals such as the wood mouse. I wonder if any of today's generation of school children split the hips to extract this most potent natural agent of itchiness. As yet the sloes of the blackthorn are much less conspicuous.

In examining the hedgerow one concludes that many plants have already seeded during the preceding months. The biennial foxglove is one such, and now the pointed seed-heads of that delightful little red flower herb robert are seen. Hedge bedstraw now producing small black seeds. For some time the leaves of wild arum, or cuckoo pint, have wilted away to expose the spadix of orange fruits.

Hogweed seed discs fall away with the winds, emptying the umbels of this tall sturdy plant. But another umbellifer, the purple-stemmed angelica, flowers much later and will not be setting seed just yet. Also still in full flower is hemp agrimony, in regiments along certain stretches of hedgerow where, needless to say, it is a prominent feature.

Suddenly there is an almost tangible feel in the air—the sword of Damocles?—very soon life, especially botanical and entomological, will be severely slain. Again we realise the preciousness of the ephemeral.

Frost is the dire foe.

No self-respecting cottage garden would be without a clump or three of Michaelmas daisies. They rank as one of my favourite garden flowers and I am in no little way enamoured of them by virtue of their magnetic draw to many insects. Even by sitting in a patio chair in a sunny corner of the garden I glean the finest detail of the various insects that amass on the flowerheads in unfrenzied feeding.

Representatives of the butterfly family *Nymphalidae*, be it small tortoiseshell, peacock, red admiral or painted lady, are a fixture; also appearing sporadically are members of the *Pieridae*, i.e. large and small white, green-veined white and in rarer instances the brimstone and clouded yellow. Hoverflies are ever present, and bumble bees, *Bombus lapidaries* and *Bombus terrestris*, are usually there in twos or threes. Oftentimes *en masse* is the large hoverfly—or drone fly— *Eristalis tenax*. Another hoverfly present is *Syrphus ribesii*. Also an unidentified black fly no more than 3mm in length.

On the flowerheads I note: the beautiful, green-washed underwings of a female brimstone butterfly; the similarly patterned antenna of the red admiral and small tortoiseshell, a saw-toothed band of white and black ending in a black knob that is tipped with white—the legs otherwise patterned: the jet 'fur' of *Bombus lapidaries:* the 'stabbing' action of the feeding hoverflies and bumble bees contrasting to the 'probing' of butterflies. A hoverfly pitches on the notepad in my hand and performs a thorough 'wash and brush-up', using its front pair of legs, as a small tortoiseshell alights on my knee.

Strategically hung from plants surrounding the Michaelmas daisies are the webs of three species of spider. A number of a small narrow-bodied fly species court danger by flying close to these webs and I spot that already some of their kind have been trapped and 'mummified'. A *'bombus'* crashes onto a web, swiftly disentangles and makes off. One of the webs, unlike the others, is of a horizontal design, and attended by what I assume are both genders of the unknown species stationed upside down underneath. What I take to be the male, smaller and seemingly full of energy darts from the centre of the web and, in short tentative bursts, twice circles the bigger female before moving back to a recent capture. It has a sky blue stripe on its 'underbelly' with white-flecked sides.

I see that, behind the Michaelmas Daisies in my garden, the clematis is seeding—just like its wild counterpart, Old Man's Beard, now beginning to feature along many of our waysides. Botanic frog-spawn.

Passivity. To the kingdom of insects particularly this is both a time of plenty but also conversely the stage where life closes perilously but inexorably on sharp decline. On observing the winged creatures sipping or dabbing flowerheads one is made aware of a blanket doggedness to get a fill and forgo all previous disposition to swift reaction. It is as if their instinct tells them their end is nigh. To illustrate this whilst blackberrying I had to shake a stem before the red admiral— in perfect condition—relinquished its meal. A silver Y moth, though, was true to form and hurtled high and away on being disturbed from a neighbouring briar.

Moths. The delta-winged mottled umber—female wingless. Lunar underwing—dark band, high abdomen. Angle shades. Figure of eight. Burnished brass, so aptly named. Brimstone. A period of wet weather can put on hold the appearance of a whole species so that one can often find specimens earlier or later than stated in guide books.

Spiders. Astronomic numbers of spiders: cropping the infinitesimal glut of insects. Just now the whole of the countryside seems swaddled in gossamer. Dew-spangled orbed webs along the hedgerow catch and refract the morning sunlight. The great majority of these are the work of the diadem spider *Araneus diadematus*—mis-named but popularly known as the garden spider. Although conceding that it is commonly found in gardens its prolific numbers can be gauged by walking alongside hedgerows where the perfect workmanship of the orbed webs mark one's every stride.

Silk plays a vital role in the life of the spider. It is used for netting and constricting prey and, particularly for the young grass spiders, used as a means of travel, of escape—the trailing thread, or dragline, enabling them to 'balloon away' on the faintest up-draught.

Cannibalism is rife in the spider kingdom and, on hatching, young spiders must evade the hungry eye of both adult and peer and scuttle quickly away from 'home'. Having successfully 'escaped' the spiderling will climb to a vantage point, throw up its hind feet, stand on its head and feed out a wide strand of silk which, hopefully, catches an air current to sweep it far away. Fascinating.

Some spider species work at night. Around the bulkhead light a dozen or so spiders await small insects and moths.

Perched, immobile, along the fencing wires are recently fledged swallows, sporting beak-length ceres (naked wax-like membranes). They appear thoroughly uninterested in the world about them but, in fact, are watching intently as their parents sweep low over the sward and jink in mazy flight about the flock of sheep. The time is rapidly approaching when the serving of insects from their parents ends and survival is laid squarely at their door.

The longer fledgling birds survive, their chances of reaching a reasonable life-span are increased. The first few months are crucial and casualties are high. They must learn quickly and obey instinct, i.e. be alert to danger and react quickly.

> The Gods approve
> The depth and not the tumult of the soul.

> A busy and aimless generation has learnt to control all forces but the tumult of its own unacknowledged soul.

> from 'The Happy Village' *Sir William Beach Thomas*

3rd Sept. 1999. The clear cries from five, cloud-high wheeling buzzards and the 'kronk kronk' of passing ravens served to emphasise the soul-satisfying serenity enwrapping the village: the blessings of quietude then overlayed with the recognised glory of soaring effortless flight. Later that same afternoon starlings from the pinnacles and battlements of the church tower were watched making frequent sallies into the open insect-filled air where they flashed and stalled catching their fill. But swallows and martins appeared and took exception to the aerial-cropping starlings, and immediately engaged them. The harried starlings were palpably surprised by the novelty of it, and back on the tower their discursive fellow *Sturnidae* were giving vent to the perplexities of the 'dog-fights' . . .

Into the second week of September and along the wayside I list the following wildflowers still in bloom. Hedge bedstraw, (a swathe of) white deadnettle, mouse-ear, ragwort (including, along the coast, silver ragwort), red campion, ragged robin (in a couple of localities), foxglove, rosebay willow-herb, bitter-sweet, tansy, St John's wort, yarrow, figwort, feverfew, golden rod, green alkanet, everlasting pea, ribwort plantain, herb robert, hedgerow cranesbill, hedge woundwort, wild carrot, wild basil, wild sage, hemp agrimony, fleabane, centuary, black medick, melilot, tufted vetch, hairy bittercress, birds foot trefoil, cinquefoil, scarlet pimpernel, mouse-ear hawk-weed, meadowsweet and yellow toadflax. The mallow struggles with a few last flowers.

And . . . the cuckoo pint.

> (The shining berry, as the ruby bright,
> Might please the taste and tempt the eager sight;
> Trust not this specious veil; beneath its guise,
> In humid streams, a fatal poison lies).

Montbretia has become naturalized in several haunts and its flowering season extends into September. The flowers of course are orange in colour and looked for by honey bees and other insects.

Ploughman's spikenard now shows. Borage also.

Sycamore and elm leaves are among the first to fall.

Now the leaves on a few hawthorns and sycamores—but on a great many hedgerow-trained oaks—are 'flour-coated' with mildew. Particularly vulnerable it seems are the leaves of the turkey oak, *Quercus cerris*. Turkey oak leaves in such sites are noted for their characteristic irregular and deeply incised leaf lobes. Mildew also on meadowsweet.

In a part of the garden lying fallow and sheltered by tall cypresses, plants of purple toadflax have attained a height of 30cm [twelve inches] and more. A young wren uses the hedging cypress as a 'boardwalk' to collect tiny insects.

Cornfields that await the scything 'bed' of the combine harvester conceal scentless mayweed and field pansy, the latter growing in time with the cornstalks but eventually barely failing to attain a matching stature. In the stubble-fields and fields of maize yet standing the black nightshade thrives.

Fat-hen (also called lamb's tongue) in the potato-fields will, in their abundance, entangle the steel arms of the mechanical diggers. In a field of maturing kale, grown as cattle-fodder and strip-grazed during the winter-time, both fat-hen and redshank are equally numerous.

On a nettle patch are espied a gathering of shield bugs, the adults are indeed shepherding their young, intriguing. Presently, one of the adults takes to the air showing its colourful hindwings. Nearby rests a scorpion fly but this carnivorous insect with its diagnostic upward curving abdomen and beak-like head and membranous (lacewing-like) wings is hardly likely to pose a threat to the well armoured youngsters, is it?

Bulges on the stalks of creeping thistle plants tell of gall wasp larvae activity therein. Pink galls on stinging nettles.

A single oak leaf can support 300 tiny insects.

Many dock leaves are brown as a result of the past feeding activity of dock leaf beetle larvae. Innumerable leaves—especially those of hogweed and meadowsweet—are, if not already targeted, being mined by caterpillars of various moth species.

One of the defining sounds of late summer and autumn—to me, and doubtless to others also—is the stridulatory music of grasshoppers, during the daytime, and bush crickets that are often heard late into the evening. In the heat of the day the mottled (short-horned) grasshoppers, family *Acrididae*, reach a musical peak, skimming away from footfall like flat stones thrown over water. The shimmer of heat and sound of grasshoppers are integral. And recourse to summers past.

Grasshoppers and crickets are insects (class *Insecta*, sub-class *Pterygota*) in the Division *Exoptergota*, which denotes there is no marked change during the life history other than size. There are some sixteen orders within this division including mayflies and dragonflies. Order *Orthoptera* (*orthos*, straight; *pteron*, a wing) represents the grasshoppers and crickets of which ten can be classed as numerous hereabouts.

On hatching the young 'adults in miniature' go through a series of moults to accommodate growth. Before the first moult the nymph is described as being a first instar. (Espied on foliage during May and early June are many grasshopper nymphs in first and second instar). Upon moulting it continues to grow and in time will require another sloughing of its skin, the nymph thereafter becoming 'second instar'. In this way its development continues until the final instar, the adult insect, after which there is no further moulting.

I have a love for the starling which perhaps some may find esoteric. Several aspects of the bird draws me. Clear 'kee-oo kee-oos' interject the babble of clucks and wheezes: positioned on the battlements and pinnacles of the church tower, and facing the westering sun the starlings, with throat feathers raised stiffly, celebrate the land of plenty spread below with (according to some nature-writers) an "artless" medley of sound which to me verily charms this hour.

> His whistle ranges from a shrill, piercing treble to a low, hollow base; he runs a complete gamut, with "shakes", trills, tremulous vibrations, every possible variation. He intersperses a peculiar clucking sound, which seems to come from the depths of his breast, fluttering his wings all the while against his sides as he stands bolt upright on the edge of the chimney. Other birds seem to sing for the pure pleasure of singing, shedding their notes broadcast, or at most they are meant for a mate hidden in the bush. The starling addresses himself direct to his fellows; I think I may truthfully say that he never sings when alone, without a companion in sight. He literally speaks to his fellows. I am persuaded you may almost follow the dialogue and guess the tenor of the discourse.

> From 'Wild Life in a Southern County' – *Richard Jefferies*

"Cack cacks" from the flock of jackdaws busily searching for corn spillage in the stubble-field. Rooks, also here, on being disturbed rise and veer away on pinion-splayed wings.

A stock dove or two are sometimes seen along the country road where corn spillage from trailers has occurred.

Midges, swarming over the marsh, produce a sound likened to 'zinging' high-power electricity cables.

In woodland, parchment-dry pendulous sedge leaves rustle against the soft breezes.

Retreating into the grassy verge a grass snake is swallowing a froglet whose shrill cries pain the very air.

The beautiful caterpillar of the pale tussock moth delights the eye. It is down from an upper branch of the birch to seek out a crevice in the bark where it will pupate. Attracted to light is the caddis fly *Phryanea grandis*, the largest of the 189 British species.

The beautiful cock bullfinch, which sampled the newly formed leaf buds of honeysuckle (and my neighbour's ornamental cherry) in my garden in late winter and early spring, again returns. This time it is accompanied by its mate, to feed on the seeds of *Aquilegia vulgaris*—that is, columbine or granny's bonnet. Although stout in build both birds sway nimbly on the slender stalks, spending several minutes at a time extracting the seed.

Walking on the raised footpath running parallel to the bank of the tidal river crane flies, by the score, buoy up from the long grass. Plants noted here at this time are white clover, devilsbit scabious and black medick and, nearer the water's edge, knotgrass, maple-leafed goosefoot and (the often rayless) sea aster. A breeze ripples the sun glistered water and effects the image of a giant silver-scaled fish.

A sandpiper streaks upriver with backflicked wingbeats and noticeable white wingbar. Under the railway bridge its 'heep-heep' alarm call is amplified. It alights on a mudflat to continue feeding in company with two grey wagtails. Shortly afterwards the birds are driven off by the tidal race—within minutes of their departure the exposed mud is several feet under water.

At the beach down to the high tide line the sea rocket shows its lilac flowers: common and frosted orache concealing greenfinches and linnets.

September is a vestige of summer when the sun is shining, a taste of winter when it rains. A vibrant hedgerow in the face of the sun becomes a spent and doleful stage in the wet. Sere bent-grasses compound the latter impression.

Bramble bushes have produced a great weight of juicy purplish-black fruit, beloved by birds, insects and man alike. Tirelessly, wasps jaw away on the blackberries, piercing through the 'outer skin' (to the advantage of many other insects with less powerful mouthparts that are similarly attracted to the banquet thereon) and ferrying portions of the fruit back to their respective 'metropolises'.

Unfortunately these selfless insects are unpopular with man and are often 'swatted on sight'. The instinct of the naturalist however is to preserve and an intrepid visitor in the home or at the picnic table is harmlessly 'guided away'. And the noble bee or wasp which stings an intruder to protect its colony sacrifices its own life—*felo de se*.

I am one with William Cowper, who lived and wrote in an age when cruelty to the higher animal order was commonplace:

> I would not enter on my list of friends
> Though graced with polished manners and fine sense
> Yet wanting sensibility, the man
> Who needlessly sets foot upon a worm.

William Cowper kept three hares as pets—as did John Clare, the Northamptonshire peasant poet—and Elizabeth Barrett Browning wrote:

> Wild timid hares were drawn from woods to share his
> home caresses,
>   Uplooking to his human eyes with sylvan tendernesses.

Death comes all too soon to vast numbers of creatures, both great and small!

Christina Rossetti's fine sentiment—

> No harmless hedgehog curled because of me
> His prickly back for fear.

—was written long before the age of motorised vehicles that slaughter, with uncompromising regularity, everything that crosses their path. (Quite apart from the environmental degradation of course). Driving the car after dark I always wince when a moth strikes the windscreen: I can only think of the intricate beauty, the delicate form that, in a split second, is extinguished. The scenario is more than an analogy to our whole treatment of the natural world, where, inured to commerce and monetary gain, humankind rushes remorselessly to what exactly? In the wake an ever mounting trail of pulverization.

> . . . And the poor beetle, that we tread upon,
> In corporal sufferance finds a pang as great
> As when a giant dies.
>
> *W. Shakespeare*

Walking along the woodland bordered country road I am suddenly amongst several beetles lumbering from one side to the other. Unceremoniously, they drag their long comb-like hind legs. I stoop to collect one and it tucks in its head, tortoise-like, and remains motionless. Now in the palm of the hand it emits a high pitched 'squeak' in response to my clasping fingers as I examine it thoroughly, noting the underside colouring of mauve shot with blue. It is *Geotrupes stercorosus*, which is smaller and rounder than *G. stercorarius*, the lousy watchmaker or 'Dor Beetle'. *G. stercorarius* is typical of hillside and woodland. But why the lemming-like impulse to cross the road in such number?

On the same day along that same road lie quantities of acorns, strangely hidden in a thick frilly ribbed case the surface of which is viscid-coated. Knopper galls, I learn later, produced by the chalcid wasp *Andricus quercuscalcis*, which was added to the British list as late as the 1960s.

Stiff wings a-rustle the impressive Emperor dragonflies hawk the hedgerows of lane and country road.

On the sloping pasture-land on the opposite flank of the stream-bottomed valley I spot horse-mushrooms in large 'fairy-rings'. I salivate: in my mind's eye these 'fruits of the ground' are already sizzling in the pan. . . .

Those puff-balls which have safely reached maturity by avoiding contact with the crushing hooves of cattle now contain trillions of spore, inviting such impact. Showing on the bracken slopes is *Hygrophorus punicous*, a blood-red fungus. Found in woodland and woodland borders the fly agaric, red with white dots, is a handsome toadstool unfailingly halting me in my tracks whenever discovered. Toadstools—and mushrooms—are the fruit-bodies of underground plants—the mycelium—which, if unimpeded, radiate from a central point to form the familiar fairy rings.

As a nature-lover I have been steeped for the whole of my life in the 'Country of the Two Rivers'. In my frequent rambles across the landscape I carry warm thoughts that many a field, footpath and lane has been likewise trodden by past generations of my family: that their rustic toil has ploughed, worked to a fine tilth and seeded the rich loam, hoed and harvested, and maintained the hedgerows. The feeling for nature which so bonds me to the country of the two rivers is distilled from those past generations. And memories, covering nearly fifty years, interplay with present experiences and blur the line between the past and the present.

Times without number have I deviated from a chosen course in order to save injury to, or avoid destruction of, some delicate work of nature—a spider's web perhaps, or a plant or insect trail . . . Moreover, I always halt my advance whenever sighting some naturally shy but alert creature —as yet unaware of the human eye upon it—ahead and take a wide berth, in order to avoid disturbance to the normal course of affairs. I always perceive myself as an ally to the kingdom of the wild; the golden rule of least disruption is obeyed.

12th Sept. 1999. Early morning I walk the path by the bank of that 'straight mile of river under the town on the Hill' so described by Williamson when setting the scene for Tarka's initial—and ultimately doomed—run from Deadlock and other members of the hound pack. That Williamson walked here, where I tread this very moment, and had observed—and later wrote intimately and with great detail about—those things I am now seeing is inspiring.

At the pathside swathes of Yorkshire Fog lie under a press of dew; and delicate-looking bents stand with their burden of sacs twinkling to the slowly rising sun. 'Jungles' of lightly perfumed Himalayan balsam—

"whose drought-roots were like the red toes of a bird"

H Williamson

—are visited by many buffish-white-thoraxed bumblebees. Pondskaters gather in the shallow, still pools by the bank: out in mid-water a small flock of swallows pass low to sip expertly at the surface, and are quickly gone.

From an open aspect the path, though still closely following the river, enters an arcade of hazel, oak and other trees. Unknowingly I have approached on an almost parallel line with three moorhens—two adults and a brown juvenile—standing on a ridge of shillet that forms a small lagoon near the opposite bank. Stock still I watch as one of the adults swims out across the river, to where my statuesque form could be seen if I showed the slightest movement. Back on the shillet the uninterested partner stretches wing and leg in unison: the juvenile meantime examines the shillet interstices. Down-river and just beyond the old railway bridge (over which the ball-clay loads once trundled, on the downward journey to the port of the little white town) a kingfisher hovers at a man's height for four or five seconds before plunging into the gliding water. With the catch wriggling vainly in its beak it flies up-river between the moorhens and the far bank, its blue-and-chestnut colouring clear. From the footings of the bridge arches a lively group of dippers also advance up-river and come to rest a few yards below the dawdling moorhens. I decide to forfeit the hour to nature's own, lest any of the birds detect my presence. Stealthily I backtrack a ways—half expecting warning notes (there are none) to abrogate the manoeuvre—before arcing away from the river scene.

The sacred queen of Night,
Who pours a lovely gentle light,
Wide o'er the dark, by wanderers blest
Conducting them to peace and rest.

James Thomson   (from 'The Seasons')

138

17th Sept. 1997. In the deep gloom of a moonless late evening, walking slow and westerly across the field. Then, at my back, the nebulous satellite—a day after its eclipse—mounts the cloud-rimmed sky. Suddenly it breaks free, luminous: my precursory shadow deepcast over tile-silver'd ground. Pleiades, my companion, oversees a realm of absolute stillness. Atmospheric. I catch myself thinking that I can spirit up the resonance of the rolling centuries: deliberate on my being of the chemistry that forms the substance of the universe. Then an owl's call frames a rare hour abroad encloaked in dark and solitude. Profound. Indelible.

19th Sept 1999. In the dell through which runs a brook there stands a mature tall crab-apple tree laden with fruit. A robin flies to it from an oak nearby and, alighting on a twig, dislodges an apple. The small fruit hits the mashy ground with an unexpectedly loud and unusual sound, to lie anonymous amongst the others already fallen. Fastened at one end to the higher branches of the tree the silk draglines of innumerable spiders hang outstretched like the wispy vapour trail of an aircraft. Lo and behold a hornet is spotted exploring the higher boughs, my first for a number of years.

27th September 1997. The day hot. On a hedgerow elm a female brimstone alighted on a leaf and listed its folded wings to catch the rays. Small copper seen. Shield bugs. Bush cricket. Ivy flowering. Still blackberrying but come the 1st October when the Devil spat on the fruits . . .

28th September. Michaelmas Day. This is the last full month for many of our migrant birds. Departing several weeks ahead of the swallows and martins, the vital swifts have left their haunts markedly subdued.

One can smell the freshly turned soil as fields of corn stubble are ploughed under, and with only the first furrows cut the tractor-driver is suddenly accompanied by the clairvoyant black-headed and herring gulls.

These and many other indications point to the fact that "the summer is gone beyond recall".

That mellow season of the year,
When the hot sun singes the yellow leaves
Till they be gold—and with a broader sphere
The moon looks down on Ceres and her sheaves;
When more abundantly the spider weaves,
And the cold wind breathes from a chillier clime.

Thomas Hood

Ceres, [mentioned in the poem above] was, in Roman mythology, the daughter of Saturn and Ops, and the goddess of corn and tillage. She is generally represented with ears of corn on her head, and holding in one hand a lighted torch, and in the other a poppy, her sacred flower.

From *Lloyd's Encyclopaedic Dictionary.*

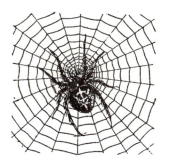

OCTOBER

Thou'rt the sunset of the year!
October is the fallen leaf, but it is also a wider
horizon more clearly seen. It is the distant hills
once more in sight, and the enduring constellations
above them once again.

Hal Borland

rion is once again high in the southern heavens, his oblique belt leading downwards to sparkling Sirius and upwards to my longtime companion on night-time sojourns, Pleiades—the seven sisters. Ah, the enduring constellations indeed.

Save for a few stragglers—one thinks here of wheatears—by month's end our spring and summer migrant birds will have departed these cooling northerly shores, the winged travellers re-crossing the English Channel on a journey south to southern and central Africa and the fringes of the Mediterranean. However, some of our sedentary bird species, of omnivorous persuasion, will be joined, especially during cold spells, by their fellow kind from more northerly latitudes than ours . . .

For several weeks now the insectivorous swallows and house martins have been gathering on the ubiquitous power and communication lines serving our towns and villages. In my old village I experienced this congregation from a thoroughly close angle. A power cable ran diagonally from the roadside pole over the lawn to a bracket on the front of my house, placed to the side of my bedroom window. For some reason the hirundines choose this particular run of cable—including, to my daily delectation, that which spanned the breadth of the window—for their morning gatherings.

141

I was chorused each morning by their excited twittering—a discussion on migration, maybe? And from the comfort of my bed I could admire the soft chestnut-throated, gleaming blue-black plumage of the swallows and the softest purest white underparts of the house martins tightly lined up as if for inspection.

For me in those heady days of early youth an exhilarating start to the day. Whenever a vehicle came through the village the flock would rise as one—'soaring into the vagueness of air'—twittering convulsively, to re-alight on the wire as light-ly as snowflakes after the intrusion as passed. Alas—these are transient times—their presence, which has brought such pleasure to the start of each (light reducing) day will soon be just a memory, as finally, a morning will be devoid of their company. Until the next spring . . .

Fondly regarded, the spotted flycatcher bids *au revoir*, to leave me once again with recollections of peace-filled hours. On several occasions over the past two months I have seen an individual in company with a mixed flock of warblers and tit-mice. The wood warblers, having given such musical enchant-ment to their woodland settings, leave us earlier than the main flow. Surrendering also to the magnetism of migration are the willow warbler and, by and large, the chiffchaff and blackcap, with whitethroat and sedge warbler.

Was it all those weeks ago when I sat watching sedge warblers on a bright cloudless early morn? It was in June and they were rising intermittently from the reeds fringing the 'drains'—near the Great Field—to perform short vertical song-flights before quickly dropping back into hiding, where even here they adminstered a few salvoes of sharp excitement.

During my childhood, farming in North Devon was, by and large, run in a traditional, holistic manner. How times have changed. A feel for the countryside and its attendant wildlife at best plays second fiddle to machine and bank balance. And the keyword is maximization of assets. Farm-hands and farm contractors hurl their giant tractors and giant machinery about the land, spraying, tilling, harvesting and hedgerow mangling as if the countryside is nothing more than a factory floor, to be wrung forcefully for its productivity. And not only by day but, with the use of power-fully beamed headlights, sometimes through the night, inflicting great stress on breeding and roosting birds.

The use of organo-phosphates on the land has not only drastically reduced insect numbers but instrumentally had the knock-on effect of sending the populations of farmland birds plummeting, including—surprisingly—the house sparrow. Would you believe that in many areas, where hersdmen administer certain potent drugs to their charges, cowpats are nothing less than sinister toxic mounds devoid of the insect-life that would normally thrive in or around this environ.

Bitter-sweet my emotions on farming. I am brooding over the mechanistic age that has befallen us, well at any rate us westerners. Farming is now on the whole a solitary occupation:

I have always held the Amish communities of North America in high regard. Their blunt refusal to submit to total mechanization is one of the salutary landmarks of the twentieth century, a pity more communities couldn't have seen the light and followed their lead—rejecting always the 'machinery hurtful to commonalty'.

If an audit were done on farming practices, on economic, sociological and ecological standpoints the bottom line would unquestionably make sober reading. As a direct result of modern farming we have pollution of our ground waters through chemical spraying, and soil compaction and erosion.

The new millennium sees farming and the countryside in crisis, which spells further degradation of our landscape. Farmers, generally through no great fault of their own, have chosen to opt out of husbandry or cereal production and diversify into other forms of enterprise. Tourism plays a major role here, with defunct farm out-buildings being renovated for summer lets or the land turned into the sterile carpets that are golf courses.

Scientific manipulation of food production goes beyond the pale: and has backfired grossly, nay grotesquely, with BSE in cattle—herbivores fed 'slaughter-house' waste—and 'god-like' dalliance in genetics giving us the cloning of an ewe

143

as well as 'modified' plant-forms. All our rich diversity of life is being put at jeopardy—why?

I feel that with each passing year something of the countryside's freshness and vitality erodes away.

Whenever I watch a ploughman at work I become an obdurate ewe. I am spellbound. There is something in the action of ploughshare biting into the rich loam and paring it into furrows which is an act as ancient as man's ascent from hunter-gatherer. The smooth crests of the furrows catch the weakening sunlight and the plough-fields gleam like seas.

The soil, the land, the countryside runs through my soul.

My great uncle was a ploughman: as a young man he ploughed with a team of shire horses, later with a tractor. Before school age I often rode on the tractor with him during the ploughing of the great 'twenty acres' field near my home.

I can remember the day when maister strode up the field and (having within the hour heard the news via the wireless) instructed my uncle of the newly-introduced law whereby the driver only was permitted on the tractor. Forthwith I could no longer accompany him from my perch on the great mudguard; a tearful schism from the world of the ploughman and his art . . .

At the edge of a stubble-field I watched a covey of eight common partridges glide in on stiff back-arched wings to settle down to feed. Although no more than thirty paces ahead of me the moment they landed I could not trace them; their colouring rendered them instantly invisible.

Letting fields lie fallow is another tradition lost to the ways of modern farming. And rotation of crops often is not observed with corn being tilled year on year on the same land. The ploughing-under of the stubble during autumntime has become a much less pleasurable sight when one considers the plight of our grain-feeding birds.

Driving along the quiet country road at first light presents one with natural history sightings that cease as the day advances and traffic is busier. At this hour the reactions of birds are not at their sharpest. I have had to draw to a halt and wait before a covey of common partridges decided to fly off, in their typical whirring manner, allowing me to continue my journey.

A first-season hare had ventured onto the road, bounded by high hedges, and on my approach sped off at an impressive rate, ignoring the possible haven of several gateways until, tiring, it accepted the invitation proffered by one some distance further along. Unfortunately a hare or two are casualty to the night-time traffic, obviously disorientated by the dazzle of headlights. Badgers too, are frequent roadside victims, particularly just after dusk. One morning I followed one well-trained fellow that lumbered along keeping tight to the hedge before disappearing up and over the bank on a well-used trail.

Another time, in October, along the same road my curiosity was aroused by spotting three recently-killed moles, each about half a mile from the last. Now what would cause this unusual event: the creatures would have had to clamber over a high hedge-bank before scuttling out onto the road—but why?

The velveted mole is both charming and mysterious. I remember being handed one when I was a lad by a farm-worker who had—mysteriously—captured one as we repaired to the edge of the wheatfield for a collective lunch break from harvesting. The harvesting was being undertaken by a trac-tor-propelled binder which cut and bound the corn into sheaves, which I was helping to 'stook'. On release the mole slipped into its natural medium, the soil, as smoothly as a diver enters water.

A daily diet of over fifty earthworms is consumed by this all-year-active fellow. And the freshly formed mole-hills across frozen iron-hard fields signify that nature's hardy specialist is down to business as usual, albeit a little deeper than in warmer days.

The maelstrom of summer life-forms has gravitated into September acquiescence to October's flensing, inexorably onward toward minimalist winter.

Insects and spiders are drawn to the sanctuary proffered by the dwelling-places of man.

The improbable flight of the cranefly parodies the flying machines of early aviators. For weeks now these insects invade all manner of locations both outdoors and, by dint of much bouncing and bumbling, the interiors of homes and buildings.

Ichneumon flies are pursuing their larval prey to the very limit of the latter's season . . .

Sowbread now shows—the flowers before the leaves, just like coltsfoot. I know of two sites where *Cyclamen hederifolium* is found. In the pinetum, around the base of the magnificent douglas fir, there is a drift and twelve miles due southwest on a roadside bank a mere two or three plants. The 5-sided throat distinguishes it from the pot-plant cyclamen.

Repullulation . . . Valiantly a few wildflowers attempt to flower anew and set seed before the Nemesis frost.

My wildflower list is much the same as September's, though of course the countryside is only sparingly populated with them.

Towering fennel now leafless. Sea rocket still in bloom. The short sea century also.

After a rain-shower the black fruit of hemlock waterdropwort fairly shine. Black fruit of wild madder and wild privet. Buckthorn and tutsan berries.

In the forest a few flowers from large-flowered hemp-nettle and angelica, nipplewort, bugle, ragwort, rosebay willow herb and honeysuckle. Siskins feeding in the tops of larches send down a steady stream of cone particles. Elsewhere larch needles rain down.

The seed purses of honesty are silk-like to the touch. Enchanter's nightshade has hooked seedbristles. A few foxgloves.

Hollyberries. Dormouse cradles a blackberry. Fox moth caterpillars plentiful. Green-brindled crescent moth.

The whistling wind swarms about the giant sycamore, pushing and pulling every bough and twig, fingering every leaf. The hawthorn is also activated like the dress of a ballroom dancer; the tree swirls to the left and then to the right, to the left and back to the right . . .

Now hear the wistful robin. Many interpret the robin's autumnal song as wistful in tone. But is it? The last three lines of Wordsworth's sonnet *The Trossachs* goes:

The pensive warbler of the ruddy breast
That moral sweeten by a heaven-taught lay,
Lulling the year, with all its cares, to rest.

In his anthology *Poems About Birds*—published in 1922—
H. J. Massingham (a nature-writer himself of great merit),
puts it succinctly:

Who can recall the tentative, half-toned meditation
of the robin's autumn song without feeling that it is indeed
adapted to the repose and evening of the year?

Birds now slip away early to roost.

Travelling by road at night one still sees a few moths and,
crossing in a dash, small mammals, mice and voles. After rain
frogs and froglets 'hop the gauntlet' to the safety of the other
side.

Nature alone is antique, and the oldest art a mushroom

Carlyle

Troops of toadstools . . . and mushrooms. I must devise a list
of those I find. There are hundreds of varieties, both in shape
and size. All arrest our attention.

Mushrooms of course arrest our attention for reason other
than the aesthetic, not that their symmetry of form is any less
than special. Like many things in nature there are good years
and not-so-good years for mushroom generation. One of the
best years ever in this area had to be 1976, the drought year.
I well remember going out with others early one morning after
the rains had finally arrived, having been told of a particularly fine place for mushrooms—near the coast—what we found
exceeded our wildest expectations.

In the instant I scaled a steep hedge-bank I thought I was
looking out into a field full of gulls: the ground lay thick with
mushrooms, so much so that one could not avoid stepping on
them. Our bags were full within minutes and it was then
home to a hearty breakfast.

Waysides hold the large parasol mushroom and the distinctive shaggy ink cap among others. Note the transitory life
of the shaggy ink cap.

147

A crimson mat of berries has formed below a roadside yew. In woodland and churchyard the berries of this venerable tree draw in the thrushes and starlings. Like the bark and foliage, the berry of the yew is poisonous. But the berry is held in a fleshy collar and this part only is palatable, so birds blithely harvest it. Once swallowed the fleshy receptacle is eventually ground and digested but not so the impervious berry, which remains intact and is passed in the droppings.

(We now know that the fruit from another long-lived, but now endangered, plant species of Mauritius benefited from the softening-up it underwent as a result of the grinding action sustained in the gizzard of the Dodo, before also being passed intact. This begs the question, does the yew have a benefiting avian association besides distribution, which in itself is an important enough factor?)

Doubtless, most of the yew trees, of varying age and height, found in our woodlands, spring up from where they landed as birds' droppings.

The yew is a remarkably long-lived tree, with some specimens said to have survived for well over 2,000 years, having been planted by heathen worshippers on sites where Christian converts later built their churches. This thin-needled, heavily branched evergreen was, in days of yore, greatly valued for its wood—the long bows used most effectively in the Battle of Agincourt were made from it. It is a popular nesting quarter and roost for a variety of birds and a useful shelter during inclement weather for the hardy rambler.

Walking along a lane I stooped to collect an acorn in its mossy cup. I looked up to admire the turkey oak towering from its hedgetop seat. (An Exeter nurseryman, J. Lucombe, was the first to plant this S. European species, in 1735). An audible gnawing swivelled my attention to the hedge-bottom opposite. I fixed my eyes to the source of the sound and stealthily approached. The sounds were intermittent, indicating the wariness of the little creature. A full minute elapsed before I spotted the wood mouse: not feeding on a hazelnut as I had assumed, but gnawing at a grass stalk. Big endearing eyes and ears are telling points to wood mouse identity. We have four mouse species: house, yellow-necked, harvest and wood. Now is the time that wood and house mice seek out human habitation.

Small-mammal watching is a fieldcraft I have still to master. Back in the summer and alongside both a woodland path and plantation-flanked road I was left hopelessly frustrated by the scurrying of mysterious tiny bodies through 'runs' in bramble, grasses and leaves.

Several times, for a ten or fifteen-minute duration, I would stand stock-still, fixing my eyes keenly on one spot of the run, awaiting a glimpse of the little parties rushing hither and thither. Plantstalks twitched, leaves rustled and high-pitched squeaks marked their trail, but as for the merest glimpse—nothing.

In every instance, even at close range, their lightning-quick and desultory movements evaded my eager eyes. I have a strong feeling that the phantom creatures were shrews, but this does not quell my sense of failure in securing an in-the-flesh view. Will next summer's bouts of obdurate staring along the footpath way finally unravel the half-mystery? Shrews must eat their bodyweight in food each day—in the case of females suckling young, half as much again—in order to stave off hunger. Lovely creatures.

The beech tree exemplifies the time of year. Its dying leaves clothe it in a gorgeous mantle, coloured with fawns, reds and browns, which is slowly unravelled and re-woven into a carpet beneath the tree—covering the seeds that have gone before.

Although also deciduous the ash does not offer too much by way of spectacle where autumnal colour is concerned, often shedding its leaves very early, long before turning to the pale yellow that would please the eye. The seeds of this tree are of course the familiar 'ash-keys'—attached to the base of the twisted wings which, when released, spin down and more often away some distance, maybe 100 yards, from the parent tree. Often many bunches of keys remain on the branches throughout the autumn and winter and into the following spring. The name ash-key dates from medieval times when door keys of that age were of a similar shape.

On a wet or overcast day a listless ash tree, with drab bunches of drooping keys, is the very mirror of dismalness.

Our wonderful natural history has provided us with invaluable native oaks—the pedunculate or common oak, *Quercus robur*, and sessile oak, *Q. petraea*, are, of course, deciduous. Of the hundreds of different species in the northern hemisphere, of which twenty or more have been introduced into this country, over half are evergreen.

The holm oak, *Q. flex*, is one such and was introduced over 400 years ago from the Mediterranean region. During the winter months its cloak of green instantly turns to silver when gusts of wind swirl the branches to reveal—by natural semaphore—the light underside of the leaves. The 'elephant hide' bark of the holm is quite distinctive.

So, as the season progresses and our broad-leaved woodlands lose their respective cloaks, a knowledge of the colour and texture of bark becomes a useful aid to tree identification. The smooth grey bark of the beech, light-coloured ash and the papery silver-coloured bark of the birch are perhaps the easiest to recognise, along with that of the sweet chestnut. The bark form of a young sweet chestnut tree consists of vertical fissures or ridges up the trunk. However, as the plant matures these become almost lateral, to form spirals that give a unique appearance. Although not a native, the eastern Mediterranean being its nearest natural home, the sweet chestnut, *Castanea saliva*, rivalling the oak for longevity, was probably brought here by the Romans, and is a more than welcome addition to our woodland stock.

The clustered berries charm the eye . . .

The fruitful stems of black bryony can vary in size from a necklace to a thick rope.

Sloes like damsons . . .

The hawthorn hedge, such a spectacle in late spring with its great froth of blossom, is now clothed in the rich burgundy of its berries. The guelder rose will continue to hold a few of its fruit throughout the month and into November.

Rain, nature's refresher . . .

There is again a certain lushness about the grasses, though my favourite, Yorkshire fog, is ever the embodiment of sappy freshness and tactility. And 'twas Yorkshire fog I sought in my young days to feed my 'jam-jarred' drinker moth caterpillars.

> Grass is the forgiveness of nature—her constant benediction . . . Forests decay, harvests perish, flowers vanish, but grass is immortal.

Ingalls (speech, 1874)

Even though we respect their priceless contribution to man's development from hunter-gatherer to agriculturalist (wheat, oats and barley were coaxed from them), we sometimes have a tendency to overlook our wonderful array of grasses and omit to consciously record their variety and habitats. Rush, sedge and bamboo are also forms of grasses.

Two noticeably tall species often found along roadside and verge are the common cat's-tail and brown bent-grass.

Couch grass is the bane of the gardener: if even the smallest section of rootstock is not removed during weeding it will quickly reshoot and extend its range, strangling the ground. It was only recently that I realised my grandfather's name for couch grass wasn't, as I had always thought, of his own rustic invention or Devonian vernacular after all, but of wider origin. He, and my father come to that, always referred to this invasive grass as 'stroil' and low and behold this label is given in the *Observer's Book of Grasses*.

Another countrified name he often used, in substitution for root, was 'more'. Again I accepted this as being essentially a Devonian corruption: not so, in *Chambers's Twentieth-Century Dictionary* I discovered this word when checking out 'the more' in its use for 'custom'. More—mor, *n.* (Spencer) a root.

(Some of the words plucked from the classics have become assimilated perfunctorily into the idiom of the artisan by virtue of house servants, stable-hands and other labourers for the—well-read—gentry at the estates.)

Unlike the robust varieties of grasses, an increasingly tenuous hold is shared by a few each of several wildflower species in token bloom, in fact almost all those that were showing during the previous month. The common toadflax, which I erroneously but abidingly call yellow toadflax, as a long flowering season and ranks high in my list of favourites. As October advances so it disappears.

2nd Oct. 1997. Four common darter dragonflies—Latin name *Sympetrum striolatum*—are seen resting on the sawn bole of a tree lying in a corner of a field and catching the afternoon sun. This species is noted for its late appearance.

One sunny early afternoon in October some four years back I happened upon eight comma butterflies resting close together on a briar. A late hatch indeed for they were all in perfect condition and, perhaps for the final time, taking advantage of an all-too-brief warming.

18th Oct. 1997. A small copper waits watchfully on the yarrow.

18th Oct. 1998. Some 190 metres above sea level and at certain points within the parish of the village in which I settled three years ago, one can see the shoulders of both our Devon moors (celebrated by many writers through the years and notably by two women, Hope L. Bourne on Exmoor and Beatrice Chase, Dartmoor). An air frost greets the day and the panoply of the heavenly firmament is clear with a sickle moon. Mid-morning, and in glorious sunshine, I took a bike ride.

South-facing hedgerows are dry, tempting reptiles to bask; a late grass snake is observed doing just that. A chirrup from overhead as, in level flight, a skylark passed over the road and then, hanging above the stubble field, delivered a short reminder of its lyrical passion.

Prevalent just now are the small 'solid wheeled' flocks of starlings each of a few hundred individuals. Soon these will coalesce to form enormous gatherings of hundreds of thousands, nay millions, of birds. The parish has healthy numbers of yellowhammers: I am keeping a watchful eye out for a Cirl's . . .

26th Oct. 1998. A damp summer is followed by an autumn notable for its wind and rain. Today there has been severe flooding in many valleys: streams have transformed into rivers, thus fed the rivers overflow their banks, forming inland freshwater floodplains.

The following day I take a ramble, heading, perchance to find otters, for a particular area where spraint had been found earlier in the year. Following the stream course some fifty yards or so up from its whitewater convergence with the broader, seemingly swifter, one, the rush of water decreases in body and sound. It is flanked by oak, birch and hazel. On a dying birch more than fifty brown bracket fungus—birch polymore—predominantly growing on its eastern side.

Disc-like spangle galls—caused by the larvae of the gall wasp *Neuroterus quercusbacarrum,* have detached from the undersides of oak-leaves and liberally sprinkle the ground. In the solitude of these natural surroundings I am at one with the world. A dipper is heard calling and in the same moment spotted, twenty yards ahead, on a narrow shelf of fine silt edging the stream. 'Curtsying' to its linear abode it wades out and submerges for several seconds before bobbing up farther upstream.

Grey squirrels everywhere: some are timid and quickly race away to the treetops, others are decidedly plucky and hold their ground, making admonishing sounds: they have reached plague proportion in the whole area.

As a boy I remember the spectacle of an otter hunt meet, and of the tall hairy-coated otter hounds that formed an abiding image. Mercifully that country pursuit has been brought to an end.

But I would be hard put to extend such sentiments unreservedly to the North American 'tree rat' stupidly introduced here (in the early 1900s in a park in Bedfordshire and, a little later released to roam the zoological gardens in Regent's Park) and, make no mistake, wreaking havoc to our native ecology by preying on birds' eggs and nestlings and stripping the bark off trees.

In the brief afternoon sunshine four species of fly, in almost equal number, cluster on the gate-post.

Any day now the Brent geese and the Scandinavian thrushes will arrive. And at October's close . . .

The falling leaves return to their roots.

153

NOVEMBER

But of all the months when earth is greener
No one has clean skies that are cleaner,
Clean and clear and sweet and cold.
(from 'November' – *Edward Thomas*)

he 1st of November. Leaves of differing shapes and shades rest on or by the embowered wood-land path following the course of the river. In a hollow, three or so metres into the wood, I notice a pool of stagnant water, partly tree obscured and further disguised by an ever thickening coat of fallen leaves. Something within urges me to take a closer look. There is movement: an aeshna (cyanea), a late southern hawker drag-onfly, is spotted. In earnest she pitches on moss covered rot-ten branches around the rim of the pool and, with a violently arched body, uses her ovipositor to probe for slender open-ings into which ova is laid. This singular encounter so late into the year elicited as much excitement as did the previous year's experience of witnessing, on the Portuguese border with Spain, a 'plague'—biblical proportions—of, not locusts, but migrating dragonflies, which swept in off the Mediterranean seaboard.

Dairy herds are now being quartered in farmyards. The beef cattle however largely remain out in pastureland and will stoically face the coming bad weather. Farmhands lug bales of hay and straw to a regular feeding spot and here the cattle rest. From such a grass flattened area comes the sweet inter-laced smell of hay and beasts so familiar to the countryman.

Box is pungent the year round.

The first ground frost 4th November. The full moon that last eve climb'd all silver is now, at 6.15 am, hanging over the western horizon, huge and golden. Within minutes it will become engulfed in the rising bank of cumulus laden with stinging cold rain that will be falling within the hour . . .

Music to the ear of the countryman is the 'chack chack' of the newly arrived fieldfares, as usual in company with the equally relished redwings. Fond reunion.

Matins from a number of birds who think that with the mild weather spring has come. Prominent in tune and duration is the 'storm cock'. Its spirited voice is heard intermittently throughout the morning, and some afternoons, from its regular tall 'stand'. Unexpected and heartening indeed, the morning salute continues from the middle of the month until way into December. Then ceases!

Brent geese are back at the estuary.

The sun's daily path is slung low in the south and fails to touch north-facing slopes white with frost.

At roosting-time one can almost set one's watch to the rooks' arrival back at the rookery. At 4pm they are almost all returned, noisily discussing the events of the day. At the same time pheasants make for their woodland roosts, stealing circumspectly from the surrounding fields to customary perches. Always a fine sight, the cock pheasants seem exotic indeed when caught in the weak sunlight and against the muted backdrop. There are both the ring-necked and the non-ring-necked. Two theories are bandied on the pheasant's arrival on these shores: was it as a result of a natural advance in territory across Europe or was it introduced, later, by the Romans during their occupation?

Green spears of winter barley showing. Ever-reliable gorse flowering. Scentless mayweed still edges a public footpath.

I am nettled by voices decrying November as a dull, miserly month. We have distanced ourselves from the natural rhythms and changing scenes of the open air.

> I welcome November as heartily as any other month. If there
> is any grayness or melancholy to be found, it must be
> in the individual; for our enjoyment of Nature or the
> reverse is largely a matter of temperament. If you
> cultivate the habit of looking for something of interest, it
> is wonderful what "grey November" will reveal.
>
> 'The Lure of the Countryside' *William Coles Finch*

Even at this 'quiet' time of the year an hour or two's walk in the countryside will soon find a notebook adorned with copious recordings.

Hazel hedgetops are bare. Most elders are bare. Last season's growth of spindleberry shoots remain green, contrasting with the general sere cloth of the hedgerows.

Although the day is stormy I must have my 'fix' of the great outdoors; I walk down the exposed country road and enter the modest airy broad-leaved woodland. There is a pleasing humic, earthy smell about the place, the melding of the organic and inorganic following leaf-fall. A hundred yards along the woodland path and one is upon a rather squat yew tree, perhaps of a mere couple of centuries' vintage. Rain-blackened by the stair-rods of downpour, it has an added gothic-sinister presence, seemingly sucking the very light out of the air. I circuit the tree and find, at eye level, small delicate toadstools sprouting from its bark! With the hint of a prickly feel at the back of my neck I move on . . .

. . . At different levels both a nuthatch and a treecreeper appear on the same tree bole, quite a frequent occurrence in my book. "Pee-pee-pee-pee" sounds the nuthatch as it leaves. A buzzard sends down particles of bark and lichen from its lookout on the top of the birch tree under which I stand; I look up as it looks down and the game is up! Away it flaps to glide over the canopy and down the deep valley with a reverberating cry. On the higher slope of the 'cover' a roe deer that must have been watching me watching the buzzard slips quietly away but today the whole animal is in sharp frame, not the usual glimpse of buff-coloured rear-end!

Fungi aplenty still: some large ground-growing types—clouded agaric and butter cap—others sprouting from decaying branches and boles. Where the track is bounded by a spring moistened stone-bank *Anthoceros laevis,* a common liverwort, flourishes.

A bark-shed ash branch echoes the facial-markings of the south sea islanders with its 'frond-like' tracery fabricated by the past burrowing activity of beetle-larvae. A 'ginger frilled' stalk, as thick as a man's upper arm, fastens and rises vertically up the trunk. This oak sleeving is ivy, which belongs to the tropical and sub-tropical plant family *Araliaceae* and is therefore unique in the British flora; much respected by this individual but often subjected to a bad press and generally scorned by country folk. . .

On the way back home the hedge-top crab apple, rain-blackened by the day's storms, could be another species entirely! Again my compulsion to brave the weather has paid dividends, the life and atmosphere of the woodland a salve to the soul . . .

After the previous week's storm, the lane that tops the wood is strewn with twigs and leaves and my (normally silent) progress is perpetually thwarted. Lying lightly on the ground is a small bright blue feather, easily identified as being the wing covert of the handsome jay. (I wonder if these are still used for making the flies used by salmon fishermen?) Almost on cue a little further ahead the owner of said feather alerts the neighbourhood of my advance by hanging 'tearing-of-linen' warning notes in the air: further on the snicking of twigs underfoot will disturb a small group of woodpigeons from the quiet business of feeding at the edge of the field flanking the lane.

Running its course through the wood the lane continues onwards towards the outskirts of the town. On the higher northern bank the elms are yearly growing to full-blown maturity, a sight to gladden the heart of any true countryman. Let us hope they continue to avoid the dreaded beetle.

The sunrise is an orange pink band along the horizon, which tinges the higher cloud banks. Near the zenith the quarter moon and planet are in close company, the Turkish flag heaven-hung!

7th Nov. Workers from an active wasps' nest use the fleeting 'windows' in the predominantly poor weather conditions to venture forth in search of supplies.

9th Nov. A specimen of red oak is bereft of leafage, whereas an English oak is still merely tinged with autumnal colouration.

13th Nov. Activity in and around the wasps' nest at the foot of the hedgebank finally ceases.

14th Nov. Wild strawberry plants tucked into the hedgebank are flowering. Also found flowering are a few each of nipplewort, yarrow, honeysuckle, herb robert and hedge woundwort—and pink purslane! Red campion will persist with a sprinkling throughout the coldest months of the year. Also a very light sprinkling of moth species now. The November moth evident.

Cassiopeia—quoins east-facing.

16th Nov. '98. For several months astronomers and night sky enthusiasts have been eagerly awaiting the 17th of this month to witness the Leonid meteorite shower as a consequence of Earth passing through the trail of debris from comet Tempel-Tuttle. Around midnight my work colleague excitedly reported he had just seen a shooting star of considerable size: our hopes were high.

We were not to be disappointed. Between 1.30 and 3.30 am we were given a celestial firework display long to be remembered. Up to fifty meteorites an hour broke through the atmosphere at varying angles. Some came in almost at the vertical whereas others hurtled horizontally high overhead. There were times when the bursting orange balls of flame seemed to be uncomfortably numerous—and close enough—as to question our safety!

The rocks hit our atmosphere at around 50,000 miles an hour but are then slowed to a mere 100 miles per hour. Consoling perhaps. How fortunate we were to witness this preview, for the following night, the long awaited 17th, proved to be a total let-down for thousands of observers as blanket cloud obscured the British night sky.

Principal meteoric showers, with the constellations from which they radiate, are as follows:

Quadrantids	Jan. 2, 3	*from*	Corona Borealis
Ursids	March 24	*from*	Ursa Major
Lyrids	April 20–23	*from*	Lyra
Perseids	Aug. 10–14	*from*	Perseus
Leonids	Nov. 13–15	*from*	Leo
Andromedids	Nov. 17–23	*from*	Andromeda
Geminids	Dec. 10–12	*from*	Gemini

Jupiter's four moons are visible through binoculars. Io, Europa, Ganymede and Callisto. Jupiter's presence in the night sky is very reassuring for its huge size—ten times the diameter of Earth—generates a gravitational pull to match, shielding the inner solar-system from rogue asteroids.

23rd November '96 was a fine day wedged between decidedly inclement ones. Through the eyes of an ardent and enthralled observer, walk with me. Along the line of the run-down hedge—why do we have so many when grants for their restoration are available?—field maple and hawthorn have been all but stripped of their leaves. Several wasps are flying about the hazel-tree which already holds small male catkins—it will be a full season before these burst out into the familiar 'lambs' tails!'

Entranced as always by the sound of stream-water. This one, doubtless like every other one in the county just now, is in spate. The mill-leat spurs from the weir where sunlight exposes a fine spray ascending from the base of the spill-over: dithering gnats appear entrapped in the vapour. Into the wood the understorey of beech saplings is in raiment of gold. Catherine's moss edges the footpath. Quiet here except for the occasional 'caw' of rooks overhead, the 'tick tick' of a wren in the scrub and 'tesip' of a grey wagtail from the bordering stream.

Out of the wood and following a public footpath back to the road I suddenly catch sight of a 'fiery furnace' on the hedgetop. It is the best possible example of a spindle-tree in berry-laden state anyone could wish to cast their eyes on. It isn't often one sees this small tree standing alone, as in this case; normally, as I find later that same walk, the spindle-tree shelters amongst other taller trees and, by this very fact, is often overlooked. The seeds are exceedingly nauseous, and so violently emetic as to have given the tree its botanical name from Euonyme (the mother of the Furies!): *Euonymus europaeus*. Like the field maple, this is another species I have long regarded with deep fondness since my first childhood forays into the countryside around me.

Looking upwards to the brow of the northward-facing hill a buzzard, with wings a-crook—facing into a stiff breeze it needs but little buoyancy—hangs almost motionless over the summit. Along the south-facing hedge are one or two each of yarrow, ragwort, knapweed, dandelion, herb robert and hogweed. Looking fresh enough to re-flower are numerous plants of Fool's parsley! However admirable these plants are, one senses they lack the vigour of those of their kind that went before. Ardour gives way to flat resignation on finding, on the dead branches of hazel, bright Coral-spot and Jew's ear!

The lane that descends to the wooded valley holds a spike of orange berries, wild arum, on its deep hank. A small flock of blackbirds are stripping a hawthorn of its berries. Ropes of red berries bespangle the hedgetop—the black bryony's fruitful conclusion.

Streams in spate carry away the remains of autumnal glory. Leaves spin and roll, submerge—into the 'clay-milt' opaqueness—and rise again to jig and sail with the fast-flowing current.

From their feeding ranges in the north Atlantic, as far north as Greenland and around into the Norwegian sea, and driven by the urge to spawn, cock and hen salmon (grilse) are now appearing in our estuaries and rivers. For several weeks the whip-like "thwacks" of their lunging bodies are audible if not always seen from the bankside as these gallant fish battle against the currents and inevitable obstacles to move up into the quieter gravelly reaches of their natal river.

Here the females excavate their 'redds' with the 'keeper' males looking on. After spawning and milting, the emaciated adults, now known as kelts, must travel all the way back into the ocean. But sharp-eyed gulls and crows feeding on foetid remains show that many do not survive the return journey!

I can recall reading a Henry Williamson short story, with a factual base, on the drowning, a long long time ago, of some local salmon-netters. On the estuary of the two rivers they

When Linnaeus (1707-1778) the famous Swedish botanist first saw the yellow flowers of the gorse or furze he fell on his knees and thanked God for its loveliness

A beech in its autumn splendour

Above : *The garden or diadem spider*

Below : *Anvil of a song thrush*

Above : A *contemporary scene harking back in time*

Below : *Simple beauty of a field rose*

Above : *A comma butterfly, warmed by an autumn sun*

Below : *Ripening spadices of wild arum*

Above : *Ivy. Flowers in autumn, berries ripen in winter*

Below : *The ubiquitous and handsome mallard*

Above : A *winter hedgerow's procreant candle*

Below : *An ever rolling stream*

Above : *Cob & thatch blend with the landscape*

Below : *Daylight's leaving*

were pulled overboard from their boats when Grampus's, in pursuit of the migratory fish became trapped in the nets deployed to catch the latter.

Grampus, a popular name for many whales, esp. the killer: technically, Risso's dolphin (*Grampus griseus*): one who puffs. (16th century graundpose, from l. *crassum piscem*, fat fish.)

Chamber's Twentieth Century Dictionary.

We have a Grampus Inn here in north Devon, the sign depicting Orca–the killer whale.

Strong winds flense the hedgerows and woodlands.

Hedgehogs hibernate. I once found one fellow in the sheltered corner of my poultry run in a 'scrape' under a thick layer of straw, as snug as you like! Some hedgehogs will still be abroad at night, often the young of the year, playing a dangerous game of chance, hoping to find enough food in these increasingly frugal times.

> Ice in November
> To bear up a duck
> Rest of the winter
> Will be water and muck!

Off the high moors red deer are elusive. That said little detective work is required to ascertain their movements and habits. In the marshy cover there is a wallow used for cooling-down and muddying of hides to protect them from parasitic insects. Fresh 'slots' in the soft mud tell of a favourite drinking spot at the streamside. A dread scene for the forester is a large swathe of conifers ring-barked by a whole herd during occupancy in the protective gloom of the plantation.

With a countryside divested of spring and summer visitors, birdwatchers are drawn to coastal and estuarine locations where phalanxes of ducks, waders and, just occasionally, geese overwinter. This said, our resident populations of, amongst others, starlings, finches, crows and skylarks are bolstered by influxes of their kind from northern and central Europe.

Irrespective of their origins, flocks of birds are now the norm—the safety in numbers concept holds firm in the avian kingdom as it does elsewhere in the natural world. Grouping separately, the endemic meadow pipits and skylarks vacate their high-altitude breeding haunts for bordering sea-level areas—but as usual, preyed on by those raptors the merlin, sparrow hawk and peregrine falcon.

A selection of nature books give accounts of a merlin vs skylark encounter whereon the intended prey slips the predator. Once, during the summertime, I too observed this drama unfold. A trilling skylark, still rising upwards into the sky, caught sight of an approaching merlin and, before the latter could strike, the now muted minstrel swiftly climbed ever higher—but the falcon remained in dogged pursuit. Suddenly the fleeing bird changed tack and, in a tight downward spiral, rapidly reached the sanctuary of the ground—its brush with death successfully over.

Various species of finch and bunting, accompanied for the winter months by the attractive brambling, gather in the stubble fields and under beech trees. And I have watched half a dozen or so yellow-hammers feeding out of the sheep troughs laid out in the open field, instantly transforming an otherwise lugubrious scene with their bright plumage. Note how, when danger threatens, yellow-hammers crouch low to the ground, partridge fashion, before taking flight . . .

The autumn and winter population of the ubiquitous starling, *Sturnus vulgaris*, is increased by immigration, and in a synchrony of movement, the enmassed swirling flocks can create vast helices, an unbirdlike spectacle. It can also invite musing on how many species, in days gone by, would have been present in similar numbers? Through disturbance and habitat loss, within the last thirty plus years the previous large flocks of wintering geese have not been seen at all in our area.

A murmuration of starlings. As I sat in a hedge facing inland to eat my sandwiches during a break from the coast-path walk with fellow ramblers, a vast flock of mostly unseen but audible starlings were feeding in the same field. How could this be? Well, both the starlings and the dense fog (each, it seemed, spreading across the whole field) were already present before our subsequent unnoticed arrival.

Some weeks before, the field had been well covered with farm-yard manure, providing sustained interest for the birds, prodding and flicking hither and thither. Every now and again a section of birds would rise, with the accompanying "whoosh" expected from hundreds, if not thousands, of pairs of wings. Flying low over our heads, the "rush" of countless unison beating wings through the veil of moisture was an exhilarating experience. And with the same exuberance the birds would wheel about and re-alight further across the field.

Incidentally, in the same vicinity, on a later November day, a green woodpecker was startled from the grassed shelf some feet below the top of the cliff-face where, presumably, it had been raiding an ants' nest. Not the kind of bird one would expect to find here—far from its arboreal home—leastways at this time of year.

The success of the starling much relies on adaptive feeding habits and a brisk knowledge of where the richest rewards are to be had. Most habitats are exploited—though a small flock flipping over beach pebbles and stones, as skilful as the turn-stones amidst them, was something I had never witnessed before, or since for that matter. With an open bill action they will often flick over the leaf litter—this time emulating black-birds—lying under trees and along footpaths, in the grey afternoon light appearing rat-like in their preoccupation. At daybreak and again towards evening, waves of starlings can be seen flying to and from their roost.

As a safeguard against predation, or simply to keep warm, numerous bird species roost communally through the winter months. In the late afternoon, one could set a watch by the cormorants' homeward flight from their fishing forays on the estuary and river to their traditional roost on the Point, some five miles away.

The numbers in a roost vary according to species. A herd (collective name) of wrens for instance, consisting of a dozen or more individuals, occupy a closed environment, such as a tree-hole or nest-box, huddling up to conserve body tempera-ture. Hundreds of pied wagtails gather on, and benefit from, the warmth percolating through the roof-top of hospital or factory. But nightly countless thousands of starlings find sanctuary in city centres or woodlands . . .

In consecutive Novembers, along both coastal and estuary paths, I have been surprised to meet solitary wheatears, seemingly without a thought of leaving our rapidly cooling climate. Black redstarts too have also been recorded lingering this late, and during the first week of November in 1993 I saw a swallow fly, eaves height, along the town's high street . . .

For the past several days the pleasing flocks of fieldfares and redwings have been eagerly awaited. The handsome Scandinavian thrushes first entered my consciousness a few months before my first ever field sighting. (My primary-school headmaster, Mr R. B. Bayliss, had given me and my fellow classmates an excellent grounding in insect study, though perhaps none were as appreciative—and fired—as I. But this specialist aspect of my wildlife open-air interest was soon overlayed by the seductive voice of—the as yet unknighted— Peter Scott and his compelling television series *Look*. Birds were soon to vie with insects as my main interest).

When, at that pre-binocular age, I first encountered a flock of these birds, I at first believed them to be mistle and song thrushes. But I wasn't certain, and my mind's eye, delving into the invaluable *Observer's Book* by S. Vere Benson, warned me otherwise. And when, with the realization of my presence, the flock rose from the frosted ground, my eyes sought points of recognition: the grey rumps of the field-fares and the crimson flanks of the redwings confirmed my suspicion.

I can still vividly recall the quiet jubilation these two 'new' species engendered within me as, noting the disappearing fieldfares' "chack, chack, chack", I climbed the gate into the rush-clumped marshland, my wellingtons scrunching the brittle ice-caps over the cattle-hoof-indented ground that the flock had just vacated.

Although they come to the UK to escape the fierce Scandinavian winter, a short spell of cold weather here will quickly prove mortal to the redwings. I remember several occasions during my schooldays when, from field and road-side, classmates retrieved their frozen lifeless bodies, and brought them in to adorn the biology table. . .

The teal is both the smallest and one of the most colourful of our ducks. Although breeding pairs remain throughout the year, numbers are vastly increased during the winter months by incomers from the continent.

At this time of year, in my walks along a certain path running parallel to the woodland stream I half expected to see a 'spring of teal' (a term wildfowlers use, describing how teal rise vertically from the water into the air). On average four or five of them frequent this locality, leaving again before winter is through.

Inland, it is a very wary species, usually allowing the observer only a fleeting glimpse of a rapid, twisting flight punctuated by a couple of 'filing-metal' "krick, krick" alarm-notes. In their winter stay on the local estuary, I have counted numbers in excess of four hundred.

Teal are dabbling ducks, and at high tide they move back from the foreshore onto the shelving sides of the creeks and guts, to preen or stand motionless for lengthy periods of time.

Here binoculars and spotting 'scope facilitate sedate observation, and the striking head colouring of the drake, together with the metallic green and black speculum (a patch on the, usually secondary, wing feathers) are quietly registered.

A bird often occupying similar inland haunts as the former is the equally wary common snipe. And just like the teal this bird is more often than not on the wing before the 'watcher of the wild' has observed its presence on the ground. On being disturbed the typical jinking flight before gaining altitude makes this bird a testing target for wildfowlers.

Many years ago an old school friend of mine showed me a snipe that he had bagged earlier that day, and although I disapproved of the unnecessary killing, I must confess to a degree of excitement at examining, in the hand, the beautiful striped and mottled plumage and, discovering for myself that its beak-tip—as an aid to catching worms when probing deep into the soil—is indeed flexible.

My first sight of a woodcock, the 'woodland snipe', was a shot specimen hanging up, for sale, outside a butcher's shop. I can still recall how I marvelled at the wonderful cryptic colouring of the poor bird's plumage. A broad-leaved woodland nearby affords me the chance to observe a pair of these fascinating birds. But normally, in other woodland localities, both coniferous and deciduous, I have no knowledge of their whereabouts until an individual is flushed up from close range, whereon the flight away is noted for its low, expertly twisting passage around the tree-trunks, with bill noticeably held downwards. The eyes of the woodcock are set high up and to the side of the head to facilitate all-round vision. An altogether fascinating species . . .

During November and December woodcock numbers are increased by immigrants from western Europe, no better time to record one; the same applying to the small jack snipe which, when flushed, does not normally attempt to put distance between it and the interloper as is the common snipe's way, but quickly drops back into cover—an action which is a good means of identification.

Traveller's joy or old man's beard *Clematis vitalba* is now forming a white mantle over hedgerow and thicket. I have read that gipsies smoked the dry stems of this woody climber, a practice the village lads (myself included) unknowingly copied—at a time when pocket money was as rare as the wryneck. The large white berries of the snowberry, a shrub introduced into the UK from North America in the early 1800s, are now showing along the edges of old gardens, hedgerows etc.

To the obvious pleasure of late harvesting honey bees, ivy now bears the familiar spiky flower crowns of greenish-yellow. A red-line quaker moth also takes full advantage. To me this climber deserves greater acclaim; too few are aware of its values. Fundamentally, it is beneficial to insects and birds and, contrary to general belief, it does virtually no harm to its tree support. The rare greenery offers a pleasing contrast to the void left by leaf-fall. On shedding its needles *Larix deciduoa*, the larch, will daub the plantation slope a pleasing red-brown.

Days of continuous rain, served from the low nimbostratus clouds, are suddenly ended and, in the now clear sky, a lone skylark hangs, to sing approval.

Absorbed in his fishing, 'old Nog' the heron stands knee-deep and motionless in the brown swirling waters of the stream. With unerring aim, the rapier bill is used to impale its prey of fish, eel, amphibian and aquatic mammals and young birds. In more sustaining times the keen-eyed bird strode about the crystalline waters, dabbing here and there at a larder full of prey. But now, after a lean hour or so, a broad, languid wingbeat propels it up over the alder-lined bank and away to the saltings, here to join others of its kind and where pickings should be richer. A heron will fish at night and I have disturbed a 'stream fisher' on more than one occasion through the years fishing in the moonlight.

In the middle section of the small river's loop (girdling the town's public park) and before its confluence with the estuary, there is a short mudflat where kingfisher and grey wagtail sometimes show. Dropping in sharply maybe a bird with narrow, white fringed wings, a redshank.

Together with 'less notable' species I have also seen here common scoter and merganser. Not a bad tally when one considers the nearness of traffic and the general public. A cormorant or two also ventures up these tidal waters, diving frequently for fish and eel. Of late, cormorants have increasingly frequented inland waters—one school of thought suggesting sea and estuary pollution to be the cause of this movement. Years ago a bounty was offered for shot birds, their fishing ability being looked on ruefully. But for centuries the Chinese, of course, used captive birds to catch fish in the most natural of ways.

After fishing out the tide, one of these birds, probably more successful than its companions, remains behind to digest its catch, and characteristically, stretches out its wings to dry. It has been propounded that the wing stretching attracts solar heat, aiding the digestion of the catch. To me this habit gives a prehistoric feel (as does a pheasant, which appears like a small bipedal dinosaur when running in the open in the weak light of an autumn or winter's day).

An absorbing hour or so has been spent watching, and timing, these diving birds through the slatted side of the timber storage shed that stands on the bank. On one occasion I was watching a cormorant when a heron came down and alighted on the opposite bank. With it being the top of the tide the heron could not possibly fish and indeed seemed content enough to stand and rest. But, within a short time, it was on the nearside bank holding a dab in its bill. Now the heron could not possibly have waded into the deep water, so what method had procured the meal?

It crossed my mind that the heron might have swooped across the water just as the cormorant surfaced with its catch and fortuitously snatched the fish en route. It did seem unlikely, but no other explanation availed itself to me. Anyway, the fish was a large one and, after a full three-quarters of an hour struggling to gulp the unwieldy fish, the indefatigable heron dropped it yet again to the ground, to get its breath before making another attempt. But just then in swooped a party of herring gulls and snaffled the prize away from literally under its nose.

VICISSITUDINOUS TIMES!

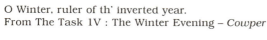

O Winter, ruler of th' inverted year.
From The Task 1V : The Winter Evening – *Cowper*

WINTER

Or call it winter, which, being full of care,
Makes summer's welcome thrice more wished,
more rare.
(Sonnet LVI) – *W. Shakespeare*

ale-raddled, the sky and sea are the colour and atmosphere that so captured the imagination of Turner, the artist. The bay itself assumes the planation of an Arctic wasteland, with its multiple troughs, though the gulls there dither lightly or rise effortlessly over splayed and ragged wave-crests in projection of some summertime idyll.

Jog on, jog on, the footpath way,
And merrily hent the stile-a,
A merry heart goes all the day,
Your sad tires in a mile-a.

W. Shakespeare

Treading our ancient circuitry of public footpaths, green lanes and bridleways makes for a palpable connection to the centuries-old journeys of our hardy forefathers, a priceless haven for those of us desirous of solitude to escape the freneticism of modern Society.

Happier life I cannot imagine than this vagrancy . . .
Nature has decreed that we must approach her shrine on foot.

De Quincey

So, no better time than now to experience (and cherish) the joys of walking, and to glory in the profound sense of

169

physical and spiritual freedom that this brings. And no better way to enhance our deep respect for the landscape, the priceless rolling countryside and to heighten our perception of its formation and structure from the mists of time, than to view it as the theatre of the history of man.

For the bared contours of our landscape inspire more than a passing interest in its geological composition and in the many stages of its development from a large glowing orb right up to the earliest chapters of human evolution.

Earth is 5,000 million years old.

The geological processes—the formation and subsequent erosion of rocks by sedimentation—are extremely slow. The ice-ages—the glacial and interglacial periods—played a key role in the formation of the land. The movement of immense ice fields scoured out deep scars from seemingly impenetrable mountains, leaving fjords and deep, steep-sided lakes.

Earthquakes, occasioned by the movement of the thin crust of surface rock as it floats on the fiercely hot, semi-liquid magma at the centre, and volcanoes, which vent the hot, liquid magma onto the surface in dramatic displays, have created more significant changes to the earth's contours.

Erosion is necessarily a drawn-out process. The repeated flow of rainwater across the soil, and against the rock, carries off a fine sediment down to the bottoms of the valleys, and out into the lakes and seas. There, storm waves add their slow attrition to the exposed littoral. The sun's heat then draws up water vapour into the clouds, later to form more rain, and the cycle repeats endlessly. But in contrast to the sudden, catastrophic upheaval caused by earthquakes, the results of erosion take many millions of years to take effect.

By the processes of erosion and the rising and lowering of sea levels, the land formed under the sea was raised up; in other areas, whole mountains became submerged, leaving but a tiny sliver visible as an island.

Around 6000 BC our south-west peninsular—as much by a rise in sea level as a drifting of the land-mass—became split from the European land-mass.

Although our peninsular escaped the southerly advance of the ice fields, much of it was once inundated, with the sea level 200 metres higher than to-day, and ice-capped seas butted the shore. Earth's features had been shaped, built up, reshaped and cut away many times before man appeared.

Half a million years ago, brute Palaeolithic man clung to his environment with a fierce tenacity. Hunter/gatherer was he, and cannibalism probably a way of life. Long extinct animals such as auroch, woolly rhinoceros, straight-tusked elephant and hippopotamus roamed. There would have been large herds of herbivores such as giant deer, reindeer, horse and bison. Seafood would have been collected from the shore-mass.

Slowly, over thousands of years, stone age man developed and adapted the techniques and skills which enabled him to secure a sound foothold on his territory. Through the Mesolithic, Later Mesolithic, the Neolithic—around 2000 BC—the quiescent Bronze Age through to the Iron Age—about 600 BC—he graduated from hunter/gatherer to sedentary pastoralist.

Man gave up his uncertain, nomadic lifestyle, and set down roots; his encampments became settlements; his artefacts surrounded him, to remind him of his nascent skills. Whole areas were appropriated, man possessed the land and began to feel the pangs of ownership; he became aware of himself, his existence, his past and hoped-for future. The door was opened to cultural progress.

Early man left his signature on a landscape thinly punctuated by signs of the long corridors of time, by means of burial sites—kistvaens (a Celtic word meaning chest of stone) where prehistoric man was buried, sitting upright with his head upon his knees, awaiting the great dawn—menhirs or standing stones, and other huge constructs. These were an affirmation of their existence by past generations living at those places, the first stirrings of a creativity that no longer came of necessity—man now yearned to design and create symbols of his new ability to think beyond where his next meal and a night's shelter were to be found.

How far we have come since those prehistoric times, when the environment had to be met 'head-on'. Today, as long as we somehow make our living off the land the environment is hardly noticed at all. Now man-made pollutants are the spur for global warming, and incidence of great disasters alerts us to the elemental and geological powers that shaped our planet aeons before our arrival.

The first lines of L.A.C. Strong's poem entitled *Frost* are:

> Unnatural foliage pales the trees;
> Frost, in compassion of their death,
> Has kissed them

Long since have those icy fingers rifled the woodland's canopy, stripped the hedgerows and laid naked almost every branch and revealing, like 'procreant candles' a veritable treasury of undiscovered birds' nests.

One can be excused for missing the lichen-covered nest of the long-tailed tit, constructed a fraction further that an arm's length into the bramble mass, and yet to have had no inkling of a wood pigeon's lattice-worked twig platform in the hawthorn a few yards farther on, well . . . .

Time to muse again on the building skills of our feathered friends. And, receiving through the post from a charity for the disabled Christmas cards painted by artists without hands, prompts me to analogy. Those indomitable artists, restricted from birth or after an accident have focused the tool for their inspiration to mouth-held brush, producing work comparable to the able-bodied.

Having adapted their upper limbs for the unquestionable advantage of flight, birds' beaks evolved into the dextrous and precise tool they employ for their everyday existence. And masterful for weaving their intricate nests.

NAKED WINTER

Beech trees, primal-looking, pencil-sketched silhouettes, symbolise the glaring starkness—and resilience—of winter. But the ash with its black buds 'shaped like the hooves of cattle' reassures us of the glories to come . . .

A TIME OF DORMANCY

The lowest pulse is the most vital!

Henry Thoreau

The metabolism of many small creatures is slowed considerably to help them sleep safely through the harshest conditions.

AND OF DEATH AND DECAY . . . and yet throughout winter's reign life forms pit their wits and energies decisively against the elements.

Nature is full of surprises, regularly furnishing exceptions to the rule. In the very depths of winter when much of our native flora and fauna are protectively encelled underground the most feebly constructed species appear, impervious to the severest conditions. Take, for instance, the winter moth: small and wingless in the female, the male flies, but weakly. To search for the 'sacrificial' females amazing numbers of males, like flurries of snow, will be abroad during the bleakest weeks: after the sharpest of frosts, the fiercest gales! Nor does heavy rainfall deter their fluttering elevation from hedgerow and woodland border. *Nota bene*—pairs of winter moths often rendezvous inside rurally sited telephone kiosks. . . .

Although the frosts have kissed the countryside many times over, the oscillating gauzy-swarms of midges will provide a spectacle (and a meal for fortunate small birds) throughout the wintertime. Normally perceived as a 'collective' organism, on capturing a midge for close examination, using a magnifying glass, as I often do to appreciate the full glory of smaller insects, this is seen to be an extraordinary delicate creation, with plumed antennae and so forth: its transparent wings can beat a phenomenal 2,000 times per second. About 150 species of midge live in the United Kingdom, the families split between the biters and the non-biters.

The shortest day arrives on 21st or 22nd December and about that time the honeysuckle bursts into leaf. Bowed, yet unscathed, the snowdrop endures the iciest blasts.

Floral seeds of regeneration lie dormant but the fauna have prepared, are preparing or will soon be thinking of the continuation of their line. The deer hinds already have life inside them and soon the vixen foxes also as the night air is pierced with the yowling of their concupiscent consorts. So filled with ardour are the dog foxes during this time my uncle tells me he was almost bowled over by one in a field as it tracked a prospective mate in the neighbourhood.

The Siberian-like conditions at the opening of the year 1997 delivered an influx of wildfowl into the estuary and the river's tidal reaches. Besides the expected sightings of curlew, lapwing, redshank and cormorant there were several of goosander, coot and tufted duck. And goldeneye, in twos and threes, entertained with frequent jump-dives. The pleading calls of the lapwings on the mudbank encapsulate the grimness of the situation: with the land ironbound the exposed and ice-free mudflats at the strandline are a life-saving habitat.

Where moments earlier a great crested grebe, uncommon in these parts, had waddled ashore and plopped down on the exposed mudflat, the tidal race was now sweeping in and repossessing the territory. With a scene more akin to the Arctic Circle, ice-sheets were lifted—amid sounds of splintering and creaking—by the fingering water and shortly afterwards sent sailing upstream on a strong and daunting current.

But the hardiness, the resilience of flora and fauna simply astound. After such testing conditions when day after day experienced sub-zero temperatures with icy blasts stemming from that inhospitable region (Siberia), there re-appeared at the point of thaw the usual—and the not so usual—life. A bat, the flittermouse of yore, was seen mid-afternoon, flying.

The springtime hedgerows will again rustle with the scurrying feet of lizards.

> Thou shalt see the field-mouse peep
> Meagre from its celled sleep.
>
> *John Keats*

And from celled sleep caterpillars will mount their foodplant, pupae hatch into butterflies and moths, wildflower seeds put forth roots and the whole world of nature, prink and vital, is again a-throb.

DECEMBER

Seneca said: When should we live, if not now?

owever discouraging the weather conditions might seem, do not give in to the artificial cosiness of indoors but get out into the invigorating outdoors. To feel centred, truly at one with myself, I need frequent and solitary sojourns into the country-side. Should the weather prove inclement, it only serves to add an extra dimension to the joys of the open air.

> "It's indoors, sir, as kills half the people, being indoors three parts of the day," says the gamekeeper. "There ain't nothing like fresh air and the smell of the woods . . . There's the smell of the earth, too, specially just as the plough turns it up, which is a fine thing; and the hedges and the grass are as sweet as sugar after a shower. Anything with a green leaf is the thing, depend upon it, if you want to live healthy."

> From 'The Gamekeeper At Home' – *Richard Jefferies*

1st December. Last year on this very day I observed a chif-fchaff busily flitting and inspecting amongst the bare branch-es of sallow and alder along the trail.

In the mud channels and salting guts alongside the tidal river, bird prints in the mud are like the reticulate veining of leaves.

2nd Dec. '92. On the saltings by the river I find the body of a great black-backed gull. There is an aluminium anklet on one leg and this bears the identifying letters BTO. I post the ring with information on the find to the British Trust for Ornithology at their headquarters in Thetford in Norfolk; a week later I receive the record of the dead bird. At nestling stage it was ringed on St Margaret's Island, Tenby, Dyfed. Here in the Taw estuary, 73 km from its birthplace and 158 days later, the hapless bird had met an early end by swallowing a discarded fishing hook and tackle.

Squabbling black-headed gulls stalk the shallows. Dunlin utter a rare 'koi koi'.

Cold weather promises the unexpected visitor to the garden.

During the winter of '62/63 I was watching, through the living-room window, the thronging birds feeding on the lawn when, to my astonishment, an albino starling flew in and joined them. It was treated with complete indifference by the other birds, although there was the inevitable squabbling when it helped itself to a morsel.

Incidentally, during that long snowbound winter I was thrilled to receive the first visits from a great spotted woodpecker. And to the farther reaches of the kitchen garden to a trench, which my father had dug for an infilling of vegetable waste in preparation for runner bean sowing, daily came a flock of skylarks.

(During that same winter I remember my English teacher, in order to inspire worthy essays from his pupils on the topic, 'snow', read two paragraphs from the chapter "The Winter Birds" in Viscount Grey of Fallodon's classic *The Charm of Birds*.

> In December the season passes from autumn into winter, and we may have a really good fall of snow. Snow is a wonderful event; the enjoyment of it is on no account to be missed. There is something exciting about new-fallen snow of any depth. Everyone knows the exhilaration with which a dog races about and plays in new snow. I have seen a tame covey of partridges show the same emotion at the first fall of snow, and play in it with every signof excitement and enjoyment.
>
> To get up on a winter morning and find the landscape made white by a heavy, quiet fall of snow in the night is like the discovery of a new land . . .

It is therapeutic scintillation from the window.

Any garden owner who regularly hangs out peanut and wild seed containers can now expect a birdwatching feast. Titmice have their own inimitable charm. Blue tits may frequent both small and the larger garden alike, and also orchards, throughout the year, often nesting there in hollows in the bole or branch of fruit trees. I once had a pair nest in a hole in the front porch of the bungalow. Nest boxes are frequently used.

The coal and marsh tits are not so forward, until the scarcity of naturally acquired food drives them to more domestic venues. Handsomely plumed, the great tit is the monarch of the tribe, always able to stir an extra thrill. The beautifully soft colours of the gentle long-tailed tit are not often seen in the garden environment but on the comparatively few occasions it does so it shows all the acrobatic prowess of its more commonly seen, and duller, cousins. Note the nervous 'in and quickly away' bird feeder visit from the marsh tit compared to the more lingering ones of blue tits.

The *Fringillidae*—finches—contribute their own special attractiveness to the garden setting throughout the year, although autumn and winter are the most reliable times to see them. Chaffinches are by and large 'pickers' off the ground, mopping up the peanut particles and seeds which drop from the feeders. They are truly lovely birds.

GOLDFINCHES

Sometimes goldfinches one by one will drop
From low-hung branches: little space they stop;
But sip, and twitter, and their feather sleek;
Then off at once, as in a wanton freak:
Or perhaps, to show their black and golden wings,
Pausing upon their yellow flutterings.

John Keats

Just recently I had for the first time the pleasure of drawing goldfinches to the peanut feeders. Hitherto they had restricted themselves to plucking the seeds from groundsel. Normally quick to flight, if perchance you sit in your car in a car park where a thistle patch happens to be, they seem not to mind a person at close quarters thus ensconced, and you will never

177

get any closer to a flock of these striking birds. (A charm of goldfinches—perfect collective noun.) Green-finches have all but made peanuts their staple diet and, like the house sparrows, are garden regulars.

Siskins are increasingly seen at garden feeding stations nowadays—pugnacious at the spoils and quite approachable at times. Linnets are not unknown to visit field-bounded gardens.

A blackbird makes a tentative approach to food scraps on the lawn, prods and backs off, then quickly advances again to procure a few more morsels before once again retreating to weigh up its position. The cock bird's black plumage—and deep yellow bill—are well known; nevertheless it is not uncommon to come across partially white birds.

I have sighted perhaps more than a score over the years with substantial lack of pigmentation, more often than not on the wings. But the most outstanding example had at least half of its plumage thus 'disfigured': a poor bedraggled fellow, set upon without the slightest warning by two and sometimes as many as five other cockbirds, to its obvious anguish. Its emaciated condition made it clear that it would not survive much further harassment.

A solicitous cock blackbird moves away from the apple permitting a hen to feed. A first year cockbird however is 'shown the door' with a drooped wing posture when it tries to help itself to a peck of the fruit.

We never miss a thing until it is no longer there. How often have we heard that said? The staid song thrush, for all the world an aloof country squire, was once a regular glad sight bounding purposefully across the lawn. Its stone 'anvil', evidenced by the empty snail shells surrounding it, was frequently met in lane and garden. No longer is this the case; song thrushes are in sharp decline in most places.

White plumage feathers on several birds suddenly seem more conspicuous. The white rump of the bullfinch for example, and the white wing-bars of the chaffinch. White outer tail feathers are a striking feature of the pied and grey wagtails and also the meadow pipit.

Along with members of the tit-tribe one of the more familiar sounds during wintertime, when the sights and sounds of the wayside are well marked—is the "peep, peep, peep" flight notes of the meadow pipit. This endearing little bird, with immaculately conservative attire and slender bill, is a common sight on grassland and grass verges alike, where it scurries about finding minute particles of food.

The debonair pied wagtail, closely related, haunts similar places as the meadow pipit, dabbing its slender little bill in rapid succession to obtain 'undetectable' things. In brief sunlight I have observed a pied wagtail fly up and snatch a cluster-fly off the side of a shed adeptly as any flycatcher. It also enjoys a bathe in water ponded in roof gutterings. Starlings are still in great voice during December and many a gardener's day has been gilded by the 'tower of babel' cackle from our sterling friend. It will not be many weeks before its plumage regains its lustre and the now dark bill metamorphoses to bright yellow.

One of my great discoveries on working through the night is the realisation that a number of birds 'sing' throughout the small hours, summer and winter alike. Suburban man will have heard, late evening, the robin singing near street-lighting. In the poplars and willows bounding the building I have heard as many as five robins singing, in total darkness. Throughout the night an almost unbroken sound from one or more of these, with occasional punctuation of bars from a songthrush. By singing I do not here mean the usual purpose or perception of this action. No: the singing, having a softer, more inquiring tone than normal daylight performances, seems to me to be better ascribed to keeping contact, reassurance of safety, equivalent to someone whistling when nervous. An antidote to fear.

The site being close to the tidal river I have also noticed how the waterbirds call out at intervals throughout the night, particularly curlews and the gull tribe. Canada geese adding their honks from time to time also. Mind you, for many years I heard as I lay in my bed the wild-free calls made by flocks of curlew flying over the moonlit roof of the house as these made their way to and from the estuary.

A strange case I here relate is of a magpie I once observed and listened to, for fully two minutes, maybe more, in a blackthorn tree bordering the trail. *Sotto voce,* the purls of sound was a soliloquy new to the listener.

At the start of an organised Ramble I reach into the recently 'thrashed' hedge to pull out a stout branch of ash—a worthy staff. With that a companion asked if I had seen *Landgirls,* the newly-released film? No, I replied. Apparently, it transpires that in one scene a hedgerow was portrayed in the mangled condition rendered by present-day mechanistic flailing. An oversight from the unsuspecting Director to make a countryman wince. With hand-twists I divest the branch of its few short side-shoots and, in so doing, a little of its bark is peeled. For the whole of the day thereafter I was treated to pleasing wafts of an aroma from the leaching sap.

Here in North Devon we are fortunate indeed to have such a varied landscape at our doorstep—proper mountains being the main exception. Our rugged coastline, however, sculpted by thousands of years of pounding waves, is a fine substitute. The cliffs provide scale and a geologic chart, just as a mountain range would.

Armed with OS map and full of zest do I walk the coastal ways. No form of encouragement is necessary to get me out on any section. At once I am inveigled by the awesome splendour of cliff scenery: an adumbration of the story of earth seen in its strata. Half observing, half musing, I am rapt in the past and present simultaneously. (A wonderful book to read, published in 1953, is S. H. Burton's *The North Devon Coast—A Guide to its Scenery and Architecture, History and Antiquities*).

The whole history of man is brief indeed when compared with the age of earth, which is around 5,000 million years old. And it is there, written in the rock faces which rear up over the Severn Sea. Shaped and reshaped many times over by surge and retreat of ice in the glacial and inter-glacial eras, the subsequent rising and falling of sea-levels and the cataclysmic forces of volcanic and tectonic plate activity from which mountains have risen and, over the millennia, been eroded away by rain, ice and wind.

My scant geology informs me that the eastern side of our area is formed of Lower, Middle and Upper Devonian rock. The Devonian was a period of shallow seas and a greatly increased land-mass, 400 million years ago, when plants adapted and evolved on the dry land and stimulated amphibian development.

The Devonian was followed by the Carboniferous period, a time when the earth's surface was subjected to uplifting, the prodigious contortions creating synclines and antisynclines—folds and over-turned folds—faults and fractures. Thus were the measures of millstone grit, and culm—Devonian for a soft sooty coal—created, covering the western half of our area as far as the Tamar valley. Claypits—the Merton basin is up to 2,000 feet deep—are faults into which sediment from erosion was washed through many millennia.

And man's history is felt along the coastline. Earthworks, Barrows and Hill-forts, constructed before and during the Iron Age are signposts to the past. Submundane minerals were the key to man's development and their prized acquisition saw trading from afar, or the overpowering of indigenous races. Fanciful it maybe to envision a time long past when Phoenicians picturesquely sailed these waters, but the sight of a buzzard sailing high above the site of a Roman signalling station is real enough. Perhaps the ancestors of this very bird looked down on the eagle-painted banners which the Mediterranean race were wont to display.

The Roman annexation of Britain occurred in 43-45 AD, but overall was hardly felt in Dumnonia, the name given for the peninsula of Devon, Cornwall and part of Somerset. North Devon figured hardly at all, for the hinterland to be traversed to reach Isca Dumnoniorum (Exeter) was heavy going and thickly wooded. The signalling station here, and others further along the coast, were put there to watch out for invaders, and in particular the Silurians, the Welsh natives, led by the chieftain Caractacus.

Last evening's weather forecast declaring sou'westerly storms arriving mid-morn had prompted me, at daybreak, to go to the Point in the hope of sighting an oceanic—or pelagic—bird or two. I arrive at the horseshoe leeward bay just as a peregrine falcon, in relaxed level flight around its course, reaches the eastern promontory arm, to settle atop a huddle of boulders. With imagery surreal, a lone cormorant sits motionless in the centre of the still sleeping, soughless bay.

As I follow the westward-leading cliff-path, eddies of an imperceptible draught levitate numerous sprigs of bracken above the steep slopes. Ahead, meadow pipits give irritated 'peep-peeps' as they rise and resettle, maintaining a safe distance.

Rounding the Point there is instant drama as the blasting wind challenges my stability. I crouch to escape its force. In no more than a stride I have left behind nature serene and face nature in fury. From shore outwards the reef broils to the pounding all-enwrapping waves. Twenty or so yards beyond this seething cauldron three small black forms—*petit penguouins*—are espied bobbing in the wave troughs.

Then, stubby wings beat frantically to propel the little auks a hundred yards to cross and ditch just to the west of the reef-tip. Aligned to these my gaze falls short to a great northern diver, which, just feet from the tumult, rolls gracefully onto its side to preen and maintain its impervious plumes.

Close by, popping its whiskered face through the furious surf, a seal scrunches its meal of crab. A theatre and players to enrich the memory forever. However, low distracting galleon clouds sweep inland, precursory to a dark forbidding wall of deluge advancing up the Channel. The forecast and the indexing of the day bisect: it is time to retrace my footsteps.

The winter months are relished for the thrill of water-bird watching at coastal, estuarine and lake settings. Always the wildfowl and waders instil a harmonious, magical atmosphere of sight and sound. And divining a palpable timelessness.

These are exciting times, who knows what the next storm or prevailing wind will bring in? Another surf scoter or black-winged stilt perhaps, or to Lundy's shores an ancient murrelet.

And, at the creek, I once viewed in close company redshank, spotted redshank and long-billed dowitcher. Eighteen eider duck, resting-up close to the shore of the inner estuary were a surprise. In the shallow water of the marsh, and unaware of my close proximity, a little egret was fishing by balancing on one black leg and stirring the silt with its yellow foot.

Occasionally a great northern diver—the very thought of which reminds me so pleasurably of the Arthur Ransome story on it, which I read so avidly in my early teens—will move into the estuary for a day or two. Well-noted is the tilt-over position, exposing the pure white underside when the bird goes through its lengthy preening process.

In the telling light conditions the jizz, the overall appearance or profile of a bird, comes unconsciously to the aid of the seasoned observer. A good guide when separating grey and golden plover is that the former seems hunched compared to the golden plover's erectness. Of course, in flight the grey plover's black 'armpit'—the axillaries—is an instant giveaway.

The purple sandpiper is 'the dunnock of the rocky shoreline' frequently overlooked in its unobtrusive search of periwinkles and the like, often in a small band.

Feeding strategies . . .

Observe how waders have developed great variance in billform to overcome competition—from the long decurved one of the curlew, sunk deep into mud, to the short one of the sanderling, used to 'stitch' the surface. The sideways sweeping action of spoonbill feeding is markedly individual. And watch how the bar-tailed godwit will sometimes 'maypole dance' its probing bill to bore deeper into sand or mud for lugworms and crustacea. Before consuming the invertebrates caught by jabbing the surface of the sand or mudflat, note how the fastidious waders, such as dunlin, race to the tideline to rinse away the clinging sediment.

Just as I included a garden bird check list (see page 24) I now provide one for the wintering waders, ducks and geese I have seen—and look forward to seeing again. As I said previously, you the Reader can match or better this list—but the essential thing is to simply enjoy observing the common and the not so common and, through the aid of your diary reflect on past warming spectacles. Enjoy the tideline scene, of feeding waders and dabbling and diving duck, punctuated by the 'curlwee' of the curlew or 'tu-tu-tu tuey tuey' of the highly strung redshank.

WATERBIRDS I HAVE SEEN along the local coastline, and around the estuary, on lake, pond and reservoir:

Anatidae—Diving duck: tufted, goldeneye, smew, pochard, eider, scaup, common scoter, red-breasted merganser, goosander.

Anatidae—Dabbling duck: mallard, wigeon, teal, shoveler, pintail, shelduck.

Anatidae—Geese, Swans: barnacle, Brent, pink-footed, Canada, mute.

Charadriidae—Plover: ringed, golden, grey, green (lapwing).

Charadriidae—others: redshank, greenshank, spotted redshank, long-billed dowitcher, curlew, knot, dunlin, sanderling, turnstone, oyster catcher, purple sandpiper, bar-tailed godwit, black-tailed godwit.

Podicipidae—Grebes: little (dipchick), great crested, Slavonian.

Moving farther afield of course one can notch up several more wintering species—I have seen avocet and long-tailed duck to name but two, in the Exe estuary. Wild swans and most of the species of geese do not reach this region as they would have in days of yore, but I have been entranced by a flock of Bewick's on the Somerset levels—where the wintering flocks of lapwings were vast. And a flock of white-fronted geese at Slimbridge, Gloucestershire were a true joy to behold. And at Chew Lake, the waterworks which supplies Bristol, I once had the good fortune to watch a bittern in a reed-bed.

One can pin-point the fields to which curlews and oystercatchers repair at high tide when estuarine or seashore feeding grounds are submerged. And the feeding pattern of most of our wildfowl is likewise dictated by, and synchronized to, the ebb and flow of the sea.

22nd December 1999—winter solstice. The full moon fairly shimmers. It is at its brightest for 133 years.

Not only does Earth's satellite play a masterful role in the eternal rhythms of life:

The earth's axis is inclined at approximately 23.5 deg to the vertical: this is called the 'obliquity of the ecliptic' and gives rise to the seasons. However, there is a slight variation in this angle, a circular 'wobble', that takes the axis from 22.1 to 24.5 deg over a cycle of 41,000 years. The fact that the obliquity of the ecliptic has a variation of just 2.4 is due to the presence of the Moon's steadying, gravitational influence. Without it, the obliquity of the ecliptic would have been much more severe; the seasons would have alternated between the unbearably hot and the intolerably frigid with great rapidity.

Alan Beher

Trees, trees, trees. God's sentinels, landmarking our lives. . .

Generations pass while some trees stand,
and old families last not three oaks

Sir Thomas Browne

It is rare for one not to have a long if not a lifelong association with a tree or trees. The horse chestnut trees, under the boughs of which in boyhood I gathered the fallen, much-prized fruits, still stand, regally dispensing memories. In my early youth I used the 'skirts' of a holly to act as a hide, observing the creatures of the mid-wood location. It too remains.

An oak, a walnut, yew and Scot's pine. The mazzard green. The sycamore where once a blackbird sang from a bough directly above me. All have a tale to tell . . .

But the two great elms which formed an arch over the road have long gone, as have the cherished apple-orchards which so imbued a happy childhood.

Nature gives to every time and season some beauties of its own.

Charles Dickens

The lower plants—unchanged from the time of their first appearance many thousands of years ago—i.e. mosses, liverworts and lichens—now are in prime condition and offering a felicitous touch of vibrant colour to winter's somewhat doleful canvas.

Representative of the ferns, namely Hart's tongue and poly-pody, are likewise plants administering relief. And navelwort too: also known as wall pennywort, the name I use for it—a succulent of the stonecrop family *Crassulaceae*. The rusty-back, similar to polypody, has dark green fronds with an underside covered in rusty-brown scales; common only here in the southwest—along many a hedgebank and wall.

Small but nevertheless eye-catching is the lichen *Cladonia floerkeana*, forming light-grey patches but with bodies like lit-tle towers which are topped bright red. Also extremely eye-catching is the agaric species *Gomphidius roseus*, which I have found in clusters growing through the pine-needled ground at the edge of conifer plantations.

In wooded areas King Alfred's cake, a black ball-shaped fungus, commonly appears on dead or dying boughs. An eye-catching species is yellow brain fungus *Tremella mesenterica*, also found on dead branches. And there are many others, of a variety of shapes and colours, awaiting an interested eye, and not all solely appear during the winter months; some, like King Alfred's cake, are a constant.

Adorning many dead twigs and branches throughout the year, is coral-spot, *Nectria cinnabarina*, with unmistakable clear pink colouring. Exposed trees particularly, standing on high ground, are often clothed in moss—or festooned with lichens.

Grass slopes are a favourite site for the yellow upright spikes of the fungus *Clavaria corniculta*.

Wildflowers too are not wholly absent and although there are always a few reminders of summertime along the wayside some are essentially of this season alone. The winter heliotrope is of this category and although a garden plant it has become naturalized in many places. Stretches of river or hedge bank have become overrun by this plant, whose leaves remain throughout the year. In a damp grove by the stream I find a colony of—now weary—herb paris which I had missed during my summertime sojourns hereabouts.

Desiccated, woody monuments stand hogweed, mullein, teasel and thistle.

In the quarry I note the gloss-green leaves of the bear's breeches plant which is now shooting up apace. Likewise the hedgerow too has its ornamentation of emerging gloss-green as scurvy grass begins to take its hold. Certain plants, we find, have adapted to and thankfully thrive on the cool wet climate afforded by winter. The guelder rose still holds a few berries.

A lambent, glowing day: the watcher relishing the interlude notices, verging the wood, a young oak standing resplendent with its full robe of rich-brown leaves. (Other types of deciduous young trees may also retain their dead leaves throughout the winter). Entering the lane into the wood something 'inert' drops from the bush, but it is a wren making off without breaking the spell of silence.

A mystery. One hawthorn stands full-laden with haws but flanked by others picked cleaned by birds? Farther on, an ominous scattering of feathers marks a blackbird's fate, victim perhaps to the talons of a sparrow hawk or the jaws of a stoat? The blackbird is normally vigilant and its clattering alarm call puts up the whole neighbourhood of small birds. I can recall more than once when I believed blackie to be scolding my advance into its territory but, instead, transpiring to be a sparrow hawk streaking-in. And every which way the pre-warned small birds scatter to safety, fractionally ahead of the accipiter's low, glancing through flight.

On virtually every country ramble one can spot the well-worn, even sunken, runs of fox and badger. There is the rank smell of fox: quite a few are seen as well. And not always obeying the instinct of the wild animal and 'clouding' its relief by keeping low, following the line of a hedge to avoid enemy eyes. Wily fox seems to know it is one hundred per cent safe to trip across the centre of the field in full view of a row of village bungalows at its perimeter. And half a mile from the local Hunt's kennels to boot!

Walking a quiet country road I can hear the soft pad, pad, pad of racing 'feet', close to the opposite side of the hedge surrounding a field of kale. With that a cock pheasant explodes into the air and loudly proclaims its alarm with a reverberant "kuc, kuc, kuc," which grows fainter as it sails away down the valley. The rambler grows accustomed, after a while, to the equally heart-pounding 'putting-up' of wood pigeon and partridge.

At dusk the pheasants, like the wood pigeons, home in to copse and plantation to roost. I have sat in wait in just such a place—a pine plantation—and watched the individuals arrive until finally I counted ten birds perched quietly overhead.

It has been said that a fox on the prowl will capture a roosting pheasant by trotting endlessly around the base of the trunk in order to make the watching bird ever giddier as it watches the circling animal. Finally mesmerised, the bird falls from its perch to provide a meal for the trickster. I have also heard of 'charming', whereby a pair or more of foxes will ostensibly play and gambol in the open, near a rabbit warren or similar den, drawing the curious prey ever closer, until it is within catching distance. Stoats are said to perform a similar trick. I have yet to witness the application of such methods but will accept that 'the history of Reynard is steeped in cunning'.

NATURE RED IN TOOTH AND CLAW

The peregrine falcon is aptly clad in the mask of the executioner; in its presence one's pulse quickens. I have witnessed any number of peregrine strikes. Once in a valley I happened to look up the very instant the stoop concluded in a great plume of feathers as the unknowing wood pigeon was rendered lifeless. And as the peregrine plucked its capture there on the slope it was heckled and taunted by a growing band of rooks, crows and magpies.

During the winter months estuarine areas are much frequented; the alluvial beds exposed at low tide are often the place to find a peregrine resting. One day with my telescope focusing on duck in a shallow pool thereabouts, with the exception of one, a pintail, they suddenly took flight. The peregrine was desirous of a meal and the pintail had been slow to make its getaway. As the peregrine swooped it squatted down into the shallow water, foiling the hunter. Time and again the peregrine attempted to snatch the duck and each time, by partly submerging, it managed to evade the talons of doom.

As the hunter's lunges slowed there appeared on the scene another of its kind. They alternated their attacks—but without success. After a further minute or so they gave up and made off—sparing the fortunate duck. (Incidentally, in bygone days the local fishermen called the pintail by the picturesque name of 'sea pheasant').

On a particularly dramatic section of coastline I remember once coming *vis-à-vis* with a peregrine as I arrived from a woodland path out onto the 'bower' standing on 400 feet of precipitous rock-face. Just yards along on the narrowest of ledges, it was facing my direction, clutching an almost featherless pigeon. Its surprise at my materialization was as discernible as mine to it: an encounter that for a brief second was frozen in time. And after its swift departure the image lingered long in the mind.

I have seen one half-stoop a kestrel that had deigned to hover over its cliff-top domain. Another time over the river I witnessed an individual playfully engage a herring gull: never have I seen such agility, panic-driven, as the large gull rolled and climbed and dived. But I decided it was only skill-sharpening on behalf of the pursuer, for it quickly lost interest and—though a breezeless summer's day—sped away with consummate ease high over the town and was soon out of sight. Another time I have seen one overhead carrying a pigeon kill and actually make a close attempt at procuring another that happened to come within range.

During some winter's night, long and dark when the twinkling vault of heaven is cloud-obscured, we might fall to recounting some past open-air joy and to voicing certain hopes for the future. Maybe the mind's eye purveys some scene from early in the day, or last week or season, or to a time in boyhood. Some past visitations to moorland or dell, woodland or Burrows richly framed in life-enhancing pleasure, eternally parrying the dross of the daily run.

Last June I found a 'mutant' foxglove. Cycling on a narrow country road, beyond the parish boundary, I happened upon a short length of hedgerow displaying foxgloves. But one was a Goliath amongst Davids, for its stout rectangular spire, at its broadest recorded a prodigious measurement of five inches. The spire was encircled, to its tip, in literally hundreds of the bell-like racemes. Fate had led me to a quite magnificent 'sport' of a plant . . .

Well do I remember in the late 1950s entering an isolated barn exploring for birds' nests, and climbing the wall-fixed ladder into the dimness of the tallat. And there, from the top corner of a stone pillar, meeting a sudden and concerted hissing which drew me back several paces. With pupils enlarging, my composure was regained simultaneous to revelation, for the 'viperous nest' was actually of young barn owls—I had found my first species that had obviated the need for proper nest-building.

I think again of birdnesting jaunts, searching for lapwing and skylark nests. And collecting and pressing wildflowers to sellotape into a sketch/scrap book. All the things that I had then considered commonplace now seem vulnerable. I haven't seen a turtle-dove in decades. Isolated growths of mistletoe have gone with the orchards that sustained them. Would that the apple orchards of my childhood re-appear.

Another boyhood memory. In my ninth summer I remember having to pass a hornets' nest at least twice a day, walking to and homeward from the primary school. The nest was at the end of the lane (leading from the farm-house at which my parents were renting rooms while we were moving house) in the gate-post which was formerly a large tree trunk. Even then, apprehension yielded to a solicitous admiration as I was compelled to close in for a sharper view of these fine insects. My hornet sightings have become few and far between. Not one has crossed my path for three years until last September 1999.

I have never forgotten the early morning walk I took one July on a track through the sand dunes which overlook the meeting of the two rivers. A commotion of birdsound was heard, coming from the marsh-meadow alongside, and peering through the marram grass tussock I saw a small flock of *passerines* mobbing a stoat. Although one can only speculate at its presence the brave small birds seemed to have deflected the 'killer' from its intended path (towards fledglings, perhaps?) and on its rapid getaway they chirruped victoriously, each to another . . .

Once on the south Devon coast an area of sea wall and foreshore was blanketed in literally tens of thousands of small insects of several orders. This could only mean that a violent up-draught of air had sucked the small creatures off the ground and, maybe, swept them at great altitude over the Channel from France?

An abiding memory too is of a crack-of-dawn walk on the moors. The heavy rain overnight made the mist-shrouded walk through the knee-high heather rather dispiriting, for leggings had been unusually overlooked and trousers therefore became quickly waterlogged. However the hour was quickly redeemed by dint of the putting-up of a brace of black grouse—a first for me—into a clearing air. Then, a glance up to the suddenly looming skyline revealed a vision. There, in silhouette, stood a noble full-antlered stag.

And hopes. That the clamour for better protection of our local natural heritage will reach such a pitch that the philistines of our society will be for ever thwarted. One would think that safeguarding the Burrows, perhaps the biggest jewel in the increasingly tarnished crown of the West Country, let alone North Devon, would be a formality, but even here it seems nothing is sacred, though the situation at present augurs well. But for much of our landscape the future remains as much in the balance as ever, and we must take nothing for granted.

Without nature we are nothing . . .

A rare open space near the town's railway station played host from late autumn throughout the winter 1997/98 to a hoopoe. What better example do we need for retaining undeveloped natural corners as a toe-hold for wildlife within built up areas.

A recently created corridor of land fenced off for the proposed downstream bridge has provided an unexpected habitat for one, if not a pair of barn owls.

An event symbolising the mysterious process and pattern of nature: out in the kitchen garden I decide to fork out the composted material from inside the home-made boarded frame and spread it over the prepared ground. Halfway down the heap I uncover several hibernating slow worms of various sizes. The dead and mouldering material becomes slightly warm to the touch—not only the catalyst for new life but protecting that which exists.

In the midst of the cabbage bed white fly rise in clouds as my legs brush the leaves in passing. A minute insect somehow withstanding the capriciousness of wintertime.

Nature charms and nature mystifies. A giant foxglove. A dead rainbow trout found in the depths of the wood. Half a dozen squirrels racing from a rabbit burrow whence a ferreter's charge had been sent. Free-range fowls, without the least experience beforehand of birds of prey, cowering from primal instinct as a buzzard at a great height appears over their run.

And: a high-pitched squeal, from either the pursued or the pursuer, diverted my attention from the nearside riverbank to that opposite. Through the dense stands of briars at the top a rabbit careered out onto the bare ledge of mud closely followed by the sinuous movement of a stoat. But, quickly sensing the exposed nature of the terrain, the stoat turned tail and retreated to whence it had appeared.

But the incident took a new turn for as the rabbit lolloped stressfully to a small hollow a carrion crow slanted in. The rabbit was pecked repeatedly. It broke away, to cover but a few yards, before becoming cornered and subjected to further fierce pecking. After several minutes of attack the rabbit summoned all its strength and made off up the slope of the bank and was lost to sight in the brambles there. I had strong doubts though that it would recover from the shock and injuries of the successive attacks.

Carrion crows can be vociferous. An individual will perch on an exposed branch and with head dipped low, then raised, send out a sharp masterful 'caark caark' . . .

Note the different approach the various bird species exhibit when going to roost. A flock of greenfinches will fly to a laurel or similar site and quickly find a perch for the night, their static forms instantly melting away into the leafy texture of the bush. However, a blackbird each roosting-time becomes agitated for several minutes and 'tolls the knell of parting day' with strident 'pink pinks' before settling down: a knell urging its feathered brethren to retire . . .?

Ivy will now be bearing a great weight of berries and these will be a source of nourishment to wood-pigeons and to over-wintering blackcaps . . .

Soon the first flowers of late winter and early spring will begin to appear: near the coast one might find an early clump of flowering snowdrops, even before December is out. The poet Thomas Ticknell (1686–1740), who wrote the lovely *The English Ideal*, labelled snowdrops 'vegetable snow.' It is questionable whether the snowdrop is a true native, even here in the West Country where it conveys every appearance of being so because evidence points strongly to its being brought here in medieval times by monastic orders. Turkey and Eastern Europe seem to be the original homelands.

Periwinkle flowers have appeared sparingly at various hedgerow haunts throughout the winter: I have found one site where, rather than the more usual bluish violet, the flowers are white.

I know of one wood where green hellebore grows: I must look for further sites . . .

Just now the wind-blasted common shows a stolid face. The common is a configuration of inclined plateaux atop three brackened slopes rich in hawthorn, oak and pine. The southern side is particularly steep and exposed, falling to the river, which glides swiftly to a knot of bridges. Running through the comparatively gentle contoured valley to the north is an alder-lined stream. The exposed roots along the shallow banks are as black as the stones in the stream-bed. In a short while the alders will, from the male catkins, take on a deep purple bloom.

The taciturnity of deep winter hones the edge of earnest spring. And . . .

In sese vertitur annus

(The years return upon themselves)

AFTERNOTES

I believe nature study to be the most rewarding hobby by far. The great joy is discovery. When I set to and wrote-up this nature journal I did not consciously make a decision to either omit or include place names of the localities relating to the particular observation (although many readers will instantly associate the Burrows as being Braunton and the Trail, yes, Tarka). Unless the species is limited to a special habitat, marine or moor, the bulk of the recordings can be generally found in greater or lesser number throughout the area. Having said that, much of the flora was recorded near sea level.

So, having been consistent throughout I will continue to be somewhat vague in describing my movements around North Devon from boyhood to manhood. The first years of my life were spent in the neighbourhood where King Aethelstan built his palace, where the River Taw is fifty feet from sea level. From here my family moved up to 'Ceital'—the Saxon place name meaning 'farm of the dwellers in the hollow'—300 feet above sea level. This I call my 'home village'. On marriage I settled in one of the four Devon boroughs formed in the late ninth century by the Saxons. Nowadays I reside again at much higher ground, in a village that was formerly a deerpark of a manorial estate. During my early childhood in North Devon, vestiges were still remaining of a past way of life which I feel privileged to have experienced.

> Where have we been, where are we now, how did we
> get here and what have we given up?

After the geological processes man has progressively shaped and adapted his environment to his needs. From his rudimentary beginnings some 40,000 years BC to the Iron Age c.500 BC the Roman annexation in 48 AD and subsequent empiric severance in c.410 through to the Saxon (and Danish) conquests c.600 the West Country and North Devon in particular has remained to a large extent rather insular and sparsely populated.

WEST
40,000—c.3000 BC Neolithic Man
c.2000 BC Megalithic Man
c.1500 BC Bronze Age Man
c.500 BC Iron Age Man
48 AD Romans
c.410 Roman Empire Severed
c.500 Migrations to Brittany. Depopulation.
c.500 Celtic Missionaries Devon
c.600 Saxon Conquest of West begins. Settlement.

In a local church history booklet I read that the aboriginals to be found in North Devon before and into the Christian era, were—correctly or incorrectly—the Cimbri. The Cimbri were an ancient Teutonic tribe originating from Jutland.

The biggest change to the area came with the building of the Link-Road (A361). Now the mores and dialect are being diluted by the amorphous mass of new settlers. Our countryside is fast disappearing.

The clergy of yesteryear had much free time, and were able to contribute greatly to our knowledge of Natural History. Gilbert White to the Rev. Mathew:

> "Times have changed. Contemporary men of the cloth
> often find themselves having to supervise the worship
> and spiritual lives of three parishes."

In my youth the vicar, Reverend Andrews (Pa'son Andrews if one lapses into dialect) wrote a running history of the parish from Saxon days for the church magazine. It was at his vicarage that we played lawn tennis, and where the illumined spotted flycatcher was encountered.

Times have also changed regarding our local bedrock of serenity. Well within my lifetime, space and peace, the very things on which I thrive, have been forfeited.

On a BBC Radio 4 programme recently I heard it said that 90% of householders in this country experience traffic noise.

From inside my modest home I can hear the skylark's melodious tunes from the surrounding fields. You cannot put a price on that. Sequestered in some rural corner a jet aircraft screaming low overhead is an unavoidable terror.

The rumble or roar of motorised traffic is anathema to me. My adopted village is, by contemporary notions, somewhat off the beaten track. The lowing of cattle or bleatings of ewes (yalls to us rustics) and lambs are the main sounds of the day here.

The permanence of nature is an anchorage from the whirlpool of modern living.

> All that mankind has done, thought, gained or been:
> it is lying as in magic preservation in the pages of books.
>
> *Thomas Carlyle*

Shortly after writing up the November section, and surmising what the area might have held in former times regarding bird numbers, I came across, in my local library, *The Birds of Devon* by W.S.M. D'Urban, FLS and Rev Murray A. Mathew, MA., FLS. published in 1895. What a treat. One is instantly made aware of the wealth of birdnotes sourced by the authors, for 'Devonshire has been the home of many eminent ornithologists' – no mean few being men of the cloth.

The Rev HG Heaven, no less, was a bird recorder and a Lundy resident from whom the authors frequently referred to when listing the sightings of that Island. The Heaven family owned Lundy Island for a time in the 1800s. Then it was referred to as 'Heaven's Country'.

An absorbing piece of information is the Rev Heavens account of the great auk's (King and Queen Murre) presence there, sometime before this bird's extinction in the 1840s. There are traditions that the white-tailed sea eagle once nested on the cliffs of Lundy, and the Osprey has had an eyrie there later than 1835. There was a great feather trade and the swarming cliffs were much persecuted by passing sailors and others and this island sanctuary was subjected to increasing disturbance through cultivation and quarrying. And summer tourists, in 'cheap excursion steamers' out from Bideford and Ilfracombe, would harry the seabirds and rob their nests.

Mr Howard Saunders, in his account of the Kittiwake (Yarrell's B. Birds, 4th ed. p653) has given a sickening history of the way in which this beautiful gull was quite recently massacred at Lundy for the sake of its wings, for which there was at the time a great demand for ladies' hats:

> "At Clovelly, opposite Lundy Island, there was a regular staff for preparing the plumes; and fishing smacks, with extra boats and crews, used to commence their work of destruction at Lundy Island by daybreak of the 1st August (when the close time under the Sea Birds' Preservation Act expired), continuing this proceeding for upwards of a fortnight. In many cases the wings were torn off the wounded birds before they were dead, the mangled victims being tossed back into the water."

The result of this cruelty was that Saunders himself had seen

> "hundreds of young birds dead or dying of starvation in the nests, through want of their parents' care; for in the heat or the fusillade no distinction was made between old and young. On one day 700 birds were sent back to Clovelly, and on another 500, and so on; and, allowing for the starved nestlings, it is well within the mark to say that at least 9000 of these inoffensive birds were destroyed during the fortnight."

The first paragraph of introduction to *Birds of Devon* also illustrates how succeeding generations saw the taming and adulteration of the landscape. Railways are the holy grail of environmentalists, but D'Urban and Mathews (and read Wordsworth's sonnet, *On the Projected Kendal and Windermere Railway*.) wrote:

> "Much might be written as to the influence of railways upon our native Fauna: they have invaded quiet bird-sanctuaries; they have rendered others accessible to gunners from a distance; they have carried the 'collector' everywhere; they have prompted and made possible the improvements in agriculture of the present day, which while they have banished some birds have conduced to the multiplication of others."

A broad-gauge track was laid through the Taw valley and the railway opened in 1854.

The Birds of Devon portrays a much wider, wilder landscape slowly but surely succumbing to drainage and clearance. It accounts a landscape that was only just beginning to feel the effects of human intervention and in particular the railways which were strongly decried as upsetting the marshland birds. Taxidermy—throughout the book the exponents of said art invariably referred to as bird-stuffers—was a thriving occupation of the day. The gun was in frequent action, being the equivalent of modern day binoculars to the 'Fathers of Ornithology'. Anything out of the ordinary, quite often the commonplace too, was shot on sight.

Birds that are now rare were in the mid to late 19th century common and conversely some of our acceptedly common species not so. The starling, also then known as the Stare (or Steer, from its cry), has greatly increased in numbers in Devonshire since about 1844: Polwhele (1797) says that starlings never breed in the county!

The siskin was rarely met; the hawfinch, as now, merely an occasional winter visitor.

Before the marshlands were drained:

> "Some thirty years ago, before the present commodious
> market-house had been erected in Barnstaple, the farmers'
> wives were wont on the market-day to set their panniers on
> either side of the HIgh Street. It used to be a matter of great
> interest to us, in those days, especially in the winter-time,
> after severe frost, to walk the whole length of the street
> inspecting the various stalls for the sake of discovering of any
> rare birds had been brought in amongst the numerous Snipe,
> Woodcock, Wild Duck, Wood-Pigeon, etc., which would be
> exposed for sale. In hard weather we should be certain to
> meet with three or four Bitterns; we have known of a dozen
> brought into the town in a single week."

Imagine my astonishment at reading an account of starlings feeding on sand-hoppers on the seashore, just as I had once witnessed, 'uniquely' as I thought, and alongside turnstones!

And the riddle of the mussel beds twisted its mysterious tail when reading, through the pages on the *corvidae*, I found that the hooded crow was said once to be a common autumn visitor to North Devon:

"...We have seen numbers of them at the mouth of the Taw at low water on the mussel-beds. In company with Herring and Lesser and Great Black-backed gulls they would be seen flying continually a short distance up into the air, and then dropping a mussel on the rocks below in order to break the shell."

Just a few years ago a 'brown' crow was resident in Combe Martin, a throwback I daresay to a long past liaison between carrion crow and hoodie. . .

Choughs, in the mid 1880s "were always to be seen on any part of the north coast between Lynton and Hartland Point, the cliffs at Abbotsham being a favourite locality". There are records of Golden Orioles nesting. . .

Rich pickings in the book for devotees of the history of our local Ornis.

I have the native's feel for the landscape

From an unimaginably hot dense fireball, 15 billion years ago, time and space began. Cosmologists have discovered that the universe is expanding, eventually we will have starless nights! One's insignificance is all too plain. Yet a summer's day spent on the Burrows or moor, meadow or woodland projects me spiritually to the centre of the universe.

My epitaph will read:
He was a man who used to notice such things.

From 'Afterwards' – *Thomas Hardy*

BIBLIOGRAPHY AND SUGGESTED READING

Songs of the Birds by Walter Garstang MA., DSc.
First published 1922 John Lane The Bodley Head
The Observer's Book of British Birds by S Vere Benson.
Published by Frederick Warne & Co, Ltd.
Photographic Guide to the Birds of Britain and Europe
by Haken Delin Lars Svensson. First published 1988
The Hamlym Publishing Group Ltd.
The Moths of The British Isles vols I & II by Richard South.
Published 1908-1980 Frederick Warne & Co Ltd.
The Wild Flowers of Britain and Norther Europe
by Richard Fitter, Alastair Fitter, Marjorie Blamey.
Published 1974-1978 William Collins Sons & Co Ltd.
The Trees of Britain and Northern Europe
by Alan Mitchell, John WIlkinson. Published 1982
William Collins Sons & Co Ltd.
Field Guide to the Butterflies and Other Insects of Britain.
Published 1984 Reader's Digest Association Ltd.
Philip's Night Sky by Patrick Moore.
Published 1990 George Philip Limited.
Tarka The Otter by Henry Williamson.
Published Faber and Faber
The North Devon Coast by S.H. Burton.
Published 1953 T Werner Laurie
The West Country by S H Burton.
Published 1972 Robert Hale & Co.
Devon by Brian Chugg. Published 1980 B.T. Batsford.
A History of Devon by Robin Stanes.
Published 1986 Phillimore & Co.
Memorials of Barnstaple by Joseph Besley Gribble (1830)
Published (1994 ed.) Edward Gaskell (Bideford)
Wild Harvest by Hope L Bourne.
Published by Aycliffe Press (Pilton)
Dicky Slader the Exmoor Pedlar Poet by J M Slader.
Published 1963 David & Charles (Dawlish)
Tarka Country by Trevor Beer.
Published 1983 Badger Books (Bideford)

Edward Gaskell *publishers*
DEVON

Reader's Notes

Reader's Notes